Douglas Dunn was born in 1942 in Inchinnan and grew up in Renfrewshire. He has won numerous awards and prizes for his poetry, including the Whitbread Book of the Year in 1985 for his book *Elegies*. He is now a Professor in the Department of English at the University of St Andrews, where he is also Director of the St Andrews Scottish Studies Institute. He lives in North Fife with his wife and two children.

by the same author

poetry
TERRY STREET
THE HAPPIER LIFE
LOVE OR NOTHING
BARBARIANS
ST KILDA'S PARLIAMENT
ELEGIES
SELECTED POEMS 1964–1983
NORTHLIGHT

drama
ANDROMACHE

fiction
SECRET VILLAGES

anthologies
THE FABER BOOK OF TWENTIETH-CENTURY
SCOTTISH POETRY
SCOTLAND: AN ANTHOLOGY

DOUGLAS DUNN

Dante's Drum-kit

faber and faber
LONDON · BOSTON

First published in 1993
by Faber and Faber Limited
3 Queen Square London WC1N 3AU

Photoset by Wilmaset Ltd, Wirral
Printed by Clays Ltd, St Ives plc

A CIP record for this book
is available from the British Library

ISBN 0–571–16963–5 (cased)
0–571–17055–2 (pbk)

2 4 6 8 10 9 7 5 3 1

Acknowledgements

Some of these poems first appeared in *Glasgow Herald, Independent on Sunday, Listener, Poetry Review, The Printer's Devil, Scotland on Sunday, Southern Review, Spectrum, Squibs* and *Times Literary Supplement*.

'Poor People's Cafés' appeared as part of *Poll Tax: The Fiscal Fake* (CounterBlast series, Chatto & Windus, 1990).

'Garden Hints', 'Australian Dream-Essay' and 'To My Desk' appeared in pamphlets published by Carniverous Arpeggio (Hull), 1993.

'"Bare Ruined Choirs"' appeared in *Somhairle: Daine is Deilbh. A Celebration on the 80th Birthday of Sorley MacLean*. Acair, 1991.

'Dressed to Kill' was commissioned by BBC South and West for the series *Words on Film*. The programme was produced and directed by Peter Symes, and shown on BBC2 in the summer of 1992. It was shot on location at Stirling Castle, Fort George, Holyrood Palace and Erskine Hospital, Renfrewshire; archive film and stills from various sources were also used. Most of the verse was written in a relatively short period close to a cutting-room if not exactly in it. I'm deeply indebted to the film's editor, Liz Thoyts, to Peter Symes, and to the cameraman, Gary Morrison, whose photography was, to say the least, obliging. I'm also grateful to Tony Mulholland for his research and helpfulness.

A few lines have been revised. Part VI of the poem was originally found surplus to requirements, but I feel the printed version is better off with its inclusion. There are extra verses in Parts XII and XIII which might help make the printed meaning clearer even if the filmed meaning is (probably) clear enough.

Contents

I

II

III

IV

V

I

Academy's Runners

I knew a philosopher once who carried a hold-all
In which he kept bricks and what looked like an old
                                        cannonball
– Lustral, obsessive, a secret and personal burden,
It punished a sin, for which there was – clearly – no
                                        pardon.

In cross-country running there's always an overdressed
                                        clown
In tackety boots, intent on a rustic renown –
You might think – though really he's there for the pain,
Kitted out with a soldierly rucksack and idiot brain.

Innocent harriers, running to give of their bests
For an hour of exertion, their teams and their glorious
                                        vests,
Don't resemble the man with the bag and agonized mind,
Or him with the weights on his feet, but they're not far
                                        behind

On the slopes, or on meadows, in rain, snow and sleet
When the whole body's knackered and ice hampers its
                                        feet.
Bedraggled in ploughland, each man feels a fool
Jiggered and comic with hundreds of lords of misrule,

Like himself, puffing and panting Corinthian sportsmen,
Though after six miles of the weather the fun's wearing
                                        thin

And it feels more like solitude's hobby, out on your own,
Working your character down to its intimate bone.

This happened one miserable wet afternoon in West
                                        Yorkshire,
A day that the climate intended for creatures with fur.
Whoever was winning, the sleet and the slopes of the
                                        Riding
Dished out to the varsity runners a bloody good hiding.

My clockwork was squeaking. Both knees turned blue
                                        and felt frigid.
My stiff upper lip wasn't stiff any more; it was rigid,
With sweat-frozen whiskers. One leg gave up its
                                        vocation.
Then I passed a duet, engaged in *fierce conversation*.

I 'dug deep', as they say; I 'put on a spurt', and I
                                        eavesdropped
On that highly peculiar discussion; and then they just
                                        stopped –
They stopped in the gestures of men in an argument.
I ran on ahead in the slush that captured each footprint

For one moment of spike-dotted grey, a small foot-sized
                                        puddle
Among fifty others that wrote on the landscape its riddle,
Its long breathless rune of the runners, a mark in the
                                        slush
That would churn in the shoes of the ruck, and melt in an
                                        after-hush.

'Fleetness of foot', oh! I ran with a 'lightness of limb',
And when I was up on a Pennine, up near its rim,
'Do something unusual,' a voice said. — I held up the wire
Of a fence for a man who was past it; and I watched him
                                                    expire

When I said, 'Isn't this *fun?*' He fell to his knees, poor
                                                    chap,
In a posture of begging: he'd never heard such crap.
It was the last thing he needed, hearing me sound so glad.
He made outrageous noises of sobbing. He'd never felt so
                                                    bad.

I ran on at the pace of a man in the jaws of perdition.
I'd finished off *someone*. Isn't *that* competition?
Not that I won, or came close to even a place in it.
Sixty-first out of hundreds, though, wasn't disgrace in it.

Vanity stinks, and I know its aroma too well,
Its selfish, competitive, cruel, malodorous smell,
Disagreeable reek, its villainous stench, sulphurous
Fragrance that gets up the sensitive nostril and does for
                                                    us.

And on that day in the wintry West Riding of Yorkshire
I thought of that man I'd met, that warped philosopher
With his hold-all of self, his intellect's furniture.
As if he was there, I said, 'Can I carry your bag, sir?'

Turn Over a New Leaf

As we undertake a decade with the customary fear
There's a rumour in the calendar that something else
                                        draws near.
A dangerous and decadent polluted twilight stalks
Depopulated cities that are numbered in our clocks.

The kicker's running on the spot
                    Before a crowded hush
Prepared to give the lousy twentieth-century the boot.
It's a run-up to Millennium.
                    Can't you see poor Clio blush? —
As she shouts across the stadium, 'No, with the *other*
                                        foot!'

Time's frantic on the planet and it lives in me and you;
It's the mother of all maggots and it's caused by what we
                                        do.
From twelve to twelve we labour round the numbers on
                                        its face;
In progress and invention we're a digital disgrace.

It's coming as a kicker runs
                    Towards a balanced ball,
A lying man's pressed fingertip, a windy afternoon
When lovers dream their children's children's
                    Children wave and call
From migrant ships that sail to stake a life beyond the
                                        moon.

O the terminated Filofax and unplugged data banks,
The notes that tell the milkman, 'No. Farewell and many
thanks';
For they've all gone off to colonize an unpolluted star
With science and technology in Noah's Abattoir.

Who then will paint the pictures?
Will they still come in a frame?
Will sculptors works in wood and stone? And will there
still be wood?
Will there still be plays and poetry?
Will each art stay the same?
Will someone still be here to say, 'It isn't any good'?

Will egos traipse across the page? Will neighbours be
malicious?
Will politicians lie for votes? Will dinner be delicious?
Honey for tea? Will philistines still bark with mockery?
Will music sound like poltergeists among the crockery?

They're the knackered, nicknamed Nineties.
They're the writing on the wall.
They're a killer virus brewing in the meadow's
microspore.
They're the weather. They're your footsteps.
They're anything at all.
It's as optimistic-dismal as Millenniums of yore.

Time's artificial corner waits where nineteen ninety-nine
Becomes a bell, a bottle and the lilt of 'Auld Lang Syne'.
Be the nice, not nasty Nineties, and nourish Man with
sense;
Be nimble, and neoteric, with nerve and innocence.

Unlike Herons

An ageing President, an Earl, two Sirs,
Three Tory Scottish Office Ministers
(And let them guess which ministers they are)
And that dry, professorial character
An air-brushed Trotsky ghosted from the snap
A Moderator in a standing nap
Three surgeons round a corpse, surrealists
A huddle of emaciated priests
They seem to meditate on troubled sex
A synod of mudflat ecclesiastics
One like a well-known local plasterer
And one the double of a TV star
A feathered gourmet and a rich physician
A really awful Labour politician
Oh my, poor heron, what will you do-oo
These foolish things remind me of you-oo

Henry Petroski, *The Pencil. A History.*
Faber and Faber, £14.99

As something to write with a pencil is cute engineering.
For how did they manage to squeeze that cylindrical lead
Into the timber to make what we all find endearing
Even when marking exams in satirical red?

Professor Petroski knows more about pencils than
                                                    anyone –
Discovery's digits, the fingers in tune with the mind,
Engineers sketching and dreaming of what can be done,
Transferring from paper to substance and something
                                                    designed.

Far back in the Freudian distance the Latin word *penis*
Crops up in its origin, meaning 'a tiny wee tail' –
Royal Sovereign, Conté and Derwent, Faber and *Venus*:
Those monarchs of pencils are not quite exclusively male.

In Primary 1 they first taught us to write on a slate.
Diminutive Romans, we formed every letter by squeak;
Then that Day of the Pencils came round – worth the
                                                    wait,
Though you sharpened them down to a stub in less than
                                                    a week.

Pencil-box Kids, each with selections of colours and Hs
                                                    and Bs;
Sweet-smelling shavings, the point that was sharp as a
                                                    dart;

A 2B for tickling the back of a neck – and how she said
                                            'Please!';
Desk-top graffiti, the sums and the juvenile art.

Computerized reason and drafting are all very well
But you can't pick your nose with a screen, and
                                        keyboards won't do
When it comes to that cedary, graphite-and-alphabet
                                            smell,
While hardware and gadgetry leave you with nothing to
                                            chew.

Ball-points and fibretips search for invented perfection
But pencils are precious as paper is. Alloy and wood –
A pencil's a symbol of making; earth grants its affection
When what man gets up to with nature is useful and
                                            good.

Petroski puts pressure on more than the point of his
                                        pencil.
'Two cultures' are One in his book. Controversy dies:
Artists and scientists using that common utensil
Dream up what they do and it's all in the same enterprise.

So read it and find out that life's a perpetual quest
For what can be decently made, and then be improved.
With stories and pictures he shows you how pencils
                                        progressed
From a stick in the sand to the mass-produced pencils
                                        you've loved.

Kabla Khun

'the visionary dreariness' — Wordsworth, *The Prelude*, Book XI

The Person from Porlock was cooking his tea
    When Coleridge rapped on his door.
'Remember? You once did the same thing to me,
    Pimpled, Porlockian bore!'

The Porlockian seasoned his Somerset stew —
    'Oh, no, sir! The honour is mine!
A pleasure to be, sir, of service to you.
    Now, sir — some laudanum wine?'

'Pander to scales and a poet's addiction!
    You damned interrupter of dreams!
What do *you* know of the still trance of fiction
    Half-written on opium's reams?'

'Ah, sir, but little, or nothing at all.
    I find what I like in Madeira.
After six draughts I'm stiff as a wall
    And my mirror reflects a chimera.'

The sky was a measureless laudanum-grey.
    It rose from an infinite sea,
Not Paradise milk, but a cloud-pewtered bay
    As real and undreamt as could be.

'Porlockian-pharmacist, how I love-hate you! —
    You sell me beginnings of vision.
Should I give you my hand, or roundly berate you,
    Or fetch you a kick of derision?

'I've strolled through the lunar and ostracized city
    Down bat-lighted ginnels of Hell,
Heard pealing in Heaven carillons of pity
    Though truthlessness rang in each bell.

'From the zeniths of God to the bottomless pit
    Such pleasures, moon-sorrows, and pain!
Eternity, deserts, and seas, and an infinite
    Abstract, horizonless plain . . .

'Moments of magical foresight it gives me.
    On Wisdom itself it enthrones me.
My terrified mind howls for peace but forgives me.
    Sell me the substance that owns me!'

'Aye, queer stuff, they tell me, strange, mystical stuff
    That modifies vision and time.
One time and place, though, are never enough
    For poets who love the Sublime.

'Am I right? Am I wrong?' he said with a wink.
    'In my youth, I, too, dabbled in verse.
In the night-time, I nibbed through whole potfuls of ink.
    I *know* of that metrical curse.

'It's heard in the scratch of the mineral pen
    Wrestling with words on the paper
When you fail to describe what you thought, yet again –
    My pen's an ignorant scraper.'

Anger shot forth from the eyes of Coleridge.
    He looked on the edge of despair
Or about to deliver English Romantic rage,
    As, roaring, he pulled at his hair.

'What are you? Who am I? And could it be true
    That the Person I need but detest
All along has been part of my being, and who
    Casts my shadow, interior guest?

'Where am I, and when? For my spirit is lost
    In the wrathfire of lies that I've told.
Ethical vagabond, in deserts of frost,
    I've been warmed where all fires are cold,

'Very cold Arctic blazes whose unmelting heat
    Releases its dancers of light
Whose movements describe all those whom I cheat
    In the ice and the salt of the night.'

'I know that my substance inspires and destroys you,'
    The Porlockian mystery said.
'I know how addiction grates and annoys you
    And how much you wish you were dead.

'But could it be true, that the meaning of you
    Depends on the meaning of *me*?
You chemical swillbowl, admit that it's true,
    And that you will never be free,

'Never, not ever, set free from your craving
    Distilled in the cauldron of mind,
Your Fancy, your Soul, and intelligence raving
    For Genius they might never find.'

'Please, don't condescend. You know who I am.
    You know what I do – but not *why*,'
Said Coleridge, sipping his minstrelsy's dram.
    'So weigh what I want and I'll buy.'

[13]

His purchase was safe in his overcoat pocket.
    He set out for home in the dark.
His mind was his own, like a face in a locket.
    Each star was an audible spark.

His shoes in the puddles made visible splashes.
    Sights turned into sounds and sounds sights.
Cobwebby winds felt like God's own moustaches
    And wrongs in the mind felt like rights.

Upside-down, inside-out, but astoundingly clear,
    He felt safe in the country called Mad
Where tomorrow is now and the far-back is near
    And good goes unchallenged by bad,

Where only the moon inhabits the present
    Along with the mind it possesses
In a city of stone composed of unpleasant
    Granite and maze-like addresses,

A city of staircases, handleless doors,
    Cul-de-sac tunnels and lanes,
Sinister engines, metaphysical floors,
    And you see someone else in the panes

Of the windows, expecting yourself – They're
                        unglazed! –
    And the noise is a grinding of clocks,
Going backwards, whose towers diminish, unraised
    By the levers of paradox.

'This is my home. – Inverted Lucidity's
    Surrender to everything! Dreams!
Poetical minds must reach out for quiddities,
    Philosophical, crystal streams . . .

'For what lies beyond what we see, and beyond
        Dreary occasions, uselessly kind
Insights to social, familiar and fond
        Life that is known; it's the mind

'That's measured and placed by all metrical writing
        Weighing our time in the language.
It's the life of the self with another self fighting.
        I say this. Samuel Taylor Coleridge.'

He stood in a field off the road, in his city.
        It was raining and not very nice.
Rain on a hedge was a county of pity.
        I'm sorry for the sacrifice.

Bedfordshire

Have you noticed the dunderheids toddling our streets
With their furtive manoeuvres, yawns, grunts and bleats,
Slouching, and shuffling, at dead slow and plod,
Somniferous, jaded disciples of Nod?

'We'd be much better off in our beds,' they all say
In a chorus that sounds like a half-swallowed yawn
Crossed with sighs of deep puzzlement, fear, and dismay,
As they dawdle and mumble and look put-upon.

There's Alice, there's Alec. – They were once very busy
Devoted to causes and not good at quitting;
But the forty-first wink's undone Alice's tizzy
While Alec's old tantrums are coddled by knitting.

'Lethargy's dormice, that's what we've chosen to be.
We're out on a supine and intimate strike.
Pass me my slippers. Pour my mandragora tea.
Inertia's lovely, and slumbering *is* what we like.'

'We happen to think that our sullen siesta's
Richly deserved, and no more than what we are due.
Damn all animation, and damn all fiestas!
'Night-'night! And, really, it ought to be bye-byes for
                                                    you.'

'The ones with velocity, business, and thrust,
Lickspittle factotums of main enterprise,
Insomniac creatures, we'll water their fidgety dust,
Then sprinkle our Morphean sand in their eyes.'

'Our country's in coma in mischievous Dreamland,
                                    ho-hum.
Torpor-led voters have chosen stagnation's
Laid-back annoyance, the gesture of sucking the thumb.
Instead of two-fingers, we give you our back-turned
                                    orations.'

'Hymn me the downy, the duvet and eiderdown,
Orthopaedic four-poster and big feather-bed,
Lyrical jim-jams and red-flannel ankle-length gown,
Significant snoozes, narcosis, the ploys of the dead.'

'Please, switch off the light. Disengage and resign.
We'll soon reach the peak of the old wooden hill.
We're reclining, defeated; we're in a decline,
Resisting what happens with naughtily negative will.'

Then they puffed up their pillows and planted their
                                    heads,
Dead to the world in their negligent beds.
Oppositional snores won't correct what is wrong,
Nor slumbering satire, nor wry cradlesong.

Libraries. A Celebration

The Mitchell, Brynmor Jones and Andersonian,
Delightful Bailey's when it lived in Blythswood Square;
The Reference Room of Paisley Public Library
And Renfrew County's branch beside the cinema —
Of thee I sing and of thy careful catalogues,
Oak tables rubbed with municipal contract polish
By dawn cleaners and anonymous mop-women.
For twenty backroom girls in Marchfield Avenue
At the unfashionable end of the book trade
I offer up these prayers to The Nine Muses
Mentioning that you did not discriminate between
Volumes by half-wits, ninnies and sparkling geniuses,
Tables of Logarithms and *The Divine Comedy*.
The Scottish Association of Assistant Librarians'
Weekend Conference at The Covenanters' Inn —
Dear God, forgive the overdose of venison
And the gluttonous bombast of beer and Beaujolais,
Intensive seminars on 'Libraries Today'.
Luminous digits of the Dewey Decimal System,
UDC and the numbers and letters of Library of
                                                    Congress,
Compute their shelf-marks on a democratic abacus;
They all go into the stacks, grammatical errors
Eating into posthumous shame like maggots
To say nothing of the acidity of lies
Or worthy thoughts that smoulder on the shadowed
                                                    shelves.
Tunes and geraniums for Akron Public Library!
Songs, too, for the lady librarians of Ohio

In white-frame rural libraries that looked like farms!
Come back, all ye enthusiasms of yesteryear
Into a retrospective ode's proclaimed rhapsodics . . .
O the joy of the clunk, opening the Compactus!
And the mischief in puncturing day-dreaming silence,
Dropping the dead-weight of Webster's *Dictionary*
Flat to the floorboards from the height of my chest.
Remember the readers, of more varieties than Heinz
Ever imagined among his alphabets of pasta,
As numerous as beans, as plentiful as soup.
The middle-aged black in Akron at his favourite table
Reading *The Journal of Negro History* end-to-end
Behind a Kilimanjaro of books on Africa
And every book written by blacks in America,
When asked what he was doing, smiled at me, and said,
'Invisible examinations on the subject of skin.
Hey, boy! You, go get me this, if you have it.'
Or the young man in Port Glasgow, studying madly
For raggedy credentials, poverty's homework,
The table-slog of his instinctive scholarship.
Or my old boss, Philip Larkin, holding a book
Written in Indonesian, published in Djakarta,
As if it were a toad that spoke back to him, saying,
'Isn't it *wonderful*? That someone *understands* this?'
Ye glossy students at last-minute mastery
In reading-rooms, posed in multiple solitudes
And making eyes at each other over the tables
In the erotic silences of scholarship!
O ye anonymous reader who marked your place
With a rasher of bacon, will I ever forget you?
O all ye ancient ladies once on waiting-lists
For Pope-Hennessy's *Queen Mary*, and little boys
Imagining armadas in Jane's *Fighting Ships*!

Philosophy and all the -ophies! Fiction! Drama!
Soft toys, soft-core, directories, encyclopaedias!
Romances, westerns, 'tec-tales, purchased by the yard!
The arts and sciences, the children's library!
All libraries at night are sleeping giants.
O ye Chief Librarians of Scotland in your good suits!
Celebrities of SCONUL, ASLIB and the *J. of Doc.*,
Associates, Fellows and Office Bearers of the Library
                                    Association,
Hear this! – the wheels of my retrieval system running
On lubricants of print and permanent devotion!

Bagni di Lucca

Elizabeth Barrett Browning

'Keeping us fresh with shadows . . .'

October's messengers have come
From up ahead, bearing invisible errands
    On September's winds.
    Visionary autumn
Performs its business as a go-between
Trusted with rumours. Numberless and green
    Upheavals shake the foliage:
There seems no limit to this land of leaves
    As ridge surpasses ridge
On misted Apuan heights where no one lives
Beyond perched settlements, a peopled air
    Founded around a sacred bell.
    The world is waving. Its *Farewell*
    Shivers in everything
    As green transacts with red,
Kindling the canopy, and wooded hills
    Promise with mottled multiples
A loveliness of leaves before they're shed.
    What can the future bring
Other than what's already lived and dared,
Written, imagined, teeming in your head,
A song to speak, but not a song to sing?
    Always, you're unprepared
For this perception of the Luccan woods
As if eternity's discovered time,
Moving against the body. Solitudes

Seethe in the timbered, many-prayered
      Rolling Apuan sublime.
      Melancholy clocks
Re-measure lifetimes now with louder tocks.
Chestnuts topple on lanes where coaches creak
With clients for the waters, roués, toffs,
Aristocratic, raffish, or antique,
      Some with their towel-wrapped coughs,
Casino fortune-hunters broken down
By dissipated appetites, excess,
      Debauchery, licentiousness,
Turning a village into Europe's town,
Its continental sickness everywhere
And autocratic laughter in the air.
      You catch sight of the truly sick
Who feel as you do for these oceanic
      Murmuring colours in the trees.
You listen as a squeaking local cart
Drowns out the chit-chat of the spa resort
      And leaf-mortalities.
Your boy paddles in the dry drifts, his hand
Held up, and only you can understand
His grasping at a leaf as others fall,
Its terrible, absurd presentiment
      Smeared on your mind, and not at all
The sort of thought with which you feel at home,
      A morbid prophecy, a hint
Depicting lyric sorrow and a leaf
Light in its falling, weightless, perfect, brief
      In its beauty, accurate
In what it makes you feel while watching it.
Aristocrats stroll from their hydrous cures,
Princelings and bankers, withered paramours

From Petersburg, Vienna, London, Rome.
  Wealth on parade, *spirituel* . . .
Imposters, swillbowls, panders, pimps and cranks,
A half-dead dandy drunk by the Lima's banks:
Political and ruthless Christendom
  Flirts with its fashionably ill.
You finger-write these truth-words on the glass —
  TREES HUSBAND POETRY DEATH
  And then erase them with your breath.
    You see a stray leaf pass
  The window where you've rubbed the pane
  Into its unnamed light again.
  Old women in the courtyard know
  What day it is. Each twig-toed broom
Scratches at time on stone-cold pools of shadow.
    There's no elbow-room
Granted by ticking clocks and passing days.
What should we do, other than write, sing, praise
The best in life and us, and being brave
With what we have, and what we do not have?
    Dusk drops Etruscan skies
On Ponte down below, where coats and hats
Stroll by the Lima. Pleasure's plutocrats,
Called by an orchestra to candlelight,
    Shall dine with wasted Dukes tonight
    On Europe of the tears and lies.

    'Oh, husband, lover, nurse,
Last year we climbed by donkey to such heights
It took no effort to caress the stars
And I felt well and strong enough to risk
A lifetime of these elevated nights
Instead of sick-beds, rooms, ink, paper and desk'.

You look around your room —
A pen, your books, a looking-glass, your comb,
        Gather to you, Elizabeth,
Portable heirlooms and unhappened death.
        Breathe on those glass words once again.
Polish the death-word with your handkerchief.
A spirit waltzes, falling, light as a leaf
        And light and lyric as the song
Sung on the street to cure you of what's wrong
Though what you hear is what the forests cry:
'Time, soon, to leave this house, and start to die'.

O bella libertà! O bella!

Australian Dream-Essay

They're selling outsize sweaters by the roadside near
                                        Coffs Harbour.
Deep-fried jacaranda blossom, candied flame-tree petals,
Appeal like hot cakes to heavy-spending Californian
                                                tourists
Driving down the length of the Bellinger valley from the
                                        weird escarpment
Searching its temperate bigness with covetous eyes.

Thousands of black fellers are conjuring up giant
                                        kangaroos,
Megapode monsters bursting free from televised fossils
To bounce towards Armidale and such towns looking
                                        for trouble.
I shut my eyes and magic shows me encyclopaedic
                                        pictures.
Thousands of Bar-Bs sizzle into action on nocturnal
                                        beaches.
In the morning their charred pocks will look like
                                        melanomas.
Surf parades with invisible, haywire percussion, the same
                                        roll
Delivered for ever with infinite watery variations.
I can hear the Pacific's micro-ticks between grains of salt.
Dawn's roisterers relax around many beach fires
Listening to one of them pull slow tunes from an
                                        accordion.

Each muscled note tells you he practises on a chest-
                                        expander.
Disco-whispers waft from the coastal pizza towns.

I walked with some black fellers and visited boulders;
I fitted my hand on secret meanderoids. They did, too;
And the boulders became red hot then burst into flames.
I got lost among megafauna, and when I found myself
Three spinsters gave me tea on their cool veranda.
They'd set sail from Glasgow a hundred and fifty years
                                        ago.
Groggy on Old Bush, I mounted my horse and headed
                                        for Nowhere.
You can get to like certain places in less than a minute.
Songs of lost loggers seeped through time's membrane.
There's much to be said for a country with Nowhere in it,
The least controversial province, peopled by mounted
                                        loners
Looking for the wandering legend of themselves and
                                        forefathers.

A large poet stood up and recited his eucalypt verses.
Only here have I seen men and women in shorts applaud
                                        poetry.
It isn't ordinary. It's both ordinary and exceptional –
Which is how it should be. His name is Les Murray.
I found myself jumping up and down with approval.
Take a time-tested language and live it on dissimilar
                                        landscapes
Far from the names and places that gave it its noise
And the shapes of the country that gave it its accents and
                                        rhythms.

Grow up saying the names of Australia and you won't be
                                                    English,
Irish, Scots, Welsh, Italian, Slav, Greek, Asian or
                                                    whatever;
You'll just be who you are with a weakening claim on
                                                    grandparents'
European or Asian nostalgia, bad blood and violence.
I like almost everyone, especially Australians.
Some of them, with several conspicuous exceptions, are
                        devoted to life, love and liberty.
What get in the way are their origins. What gets in the
                                                    way is us.
Grant them a deserved identity, and they'll teach us
                                                    something.
It will be in a version of our over-used and very tired
                                                    language.

II

Disenchantments

'It is a world, perhaps; but there's another.' – Edwin Muir

I

Microbiologizing love, despair,
Delight, bountiful dregs, the pulse can stick
On its heirloom heartbeat. The wear-and-tear

Inherited by who-we-are, echoic
Molecular chronology, begins
At birth. Congenital, genetic,

Against know-nothing, careless inclinations,
Death starts with prophecies half-heard in dreams'
Instinctive narratives. A life's toxins –

Psycho-pollution, maverick spiremes –
Gather like gut-data in the underjoyed
Body's puddles, sponges, muscles, pumps and streams.

All sorts of nastiness lead to the void
On wheels of rotten luck or bad habits,
Cirrhosis, hepatitis B, typhoid,

Mournful *-omas*, murder's vast whodunnits;
Or what we do, or what is done to us,
Those little treacheries, the scolds and frets

Being alive receives from generous
Distributors of selfishness. Over
And over, these can really do for us

As much as age. Competitive disfavour
Churns in the psycho-clock's vascular closet,
Timing private sickness, undercover

Birthday chronometers, almost illicit,
They are so personal; and they contain
Everything, seasons, sky, and the explicit

Derivatives of love, delight, fear, pain,
Betrayals, disappointments. Hereafter
Looks like sacred vision; but it's profane —

God's salesmanship, then His religious laughter.

II

The dead can't talk, or appear on your doorstep,
Or be discovered turning to you from
Beautiful landscapes, wearing smiles of courtship,

Perusals of what you've written about them.
Only in life's interior extra sense
Are they glimpsed, tending a geranium

While gathered strangely into a presence
Reality shudders at, holding off
Memory's insult to the intelligence.

Walking out of the light, a breeze's puff
By a window, you might think, where blue
Silvers on glass; and that could be enough

By itself, but someone's looking at you,
Real and unreal, inside you and outside,
A figment of the dead, the past, but true,

No matter dithering agnostic pride
Saying, 'What-is most certainly *is-not*,
But, if you must, it *might* be clarified

'By that misplaced and found-again snapshot,
That placemark concert-ticket, old days
Remembered by a pleasure that you bought

'Together in another time, always
Enslaved by the sudden, and overthrown
By unbecoming rediscoveries.'

I can make contact through the gramophone
Via Duke Ellington. So, am I mad?
Or, as the man says, am I merely prone

To accidental confabs with the dead
On the ghost-line, splicing the mainbrace
With brimful goblets of Burgundy red

While breathy missives wing through inner space?
'Don't bug me, friend. I've got a rendezvous
To keep with the transfigured commonplace.'

'It's then we think we see God. Which isn't true.
Or when you see your past objectified.'
'If anything, it's when God looks at you,

'Or who-you-were is walking by your side,
Half-meaningful, half-meaningless, but clear,
Past-self and present matching stride for stride.'

A window dribbles with a double tear.

Hereafter? No, the here and now, wonders
Far from a window's figurative thaws.
How mind moves leads the spirit into blunders

Against the grain of life and all its laws.
Hereafter? Yes, but it's in memory.
Lifetimes like loose and lacy gauze

Float through their weightless doors and fly away
When light lies like a creature on the floor
And life hereafter seems an ordinary

Conclusion to be drawn. It's not décor
For healed broken-hearts, nor occult stasis
Cultured by fairy-tale enchanted lore

From self-inflicted schizo-Christian praxis –
It happens in the eye and intellect.
Life tells you that it doesn't, but it does.

And so we say it's something we suspect
Can happen, but when it does, we turn away,
Convinced experience is incorrect

Or that the weather's curdled Saturday
Into phenomena of foliage,
Water, sky, explicable, but too risky

To ask your mind to cross an unsafe bridge
Between its preconceptions and the sense
Cradled in other realms in wordless language,

Preferring a quotidian self-defence
Against time's birdsung waggishness and tricks,
Eavesdropping on a dialect with no tense.

Ignoring, too, who caused those sudden physics.
Neglecting, also, feeling, and a brief
Inveiglement from life beyond its ethics.

Turning your back on yourself. Shunning grief.

IV

Sky and the Firth become five flying swans.
It might as well be the twelfth century –
There's nothing on the eye other than bygones,

Nothing 'modern' (whatever that might be)
To wreck a day's half-finished wilderness
Or undermine a moment's witchery.

My eyes wear glass. Twentieth-century dress
All over me, but mediaeval thinking
For several minutes as I retrogress

Into preposterous ancestry's winking
Annals and declarations. Pine-cones, thorns,
Cathedral silence and monastic drinking,

Pre-Reformation winds, primaeval ferns,
Scrub-scratchy woodlands and druidic oaks,
Show antique Scotland. Static me unlearns

Feral history, and shuns its tribal jokes,
Learning instead – truly, it feels like loss –
Identity, while distant stubble smokes

Against eternal blue. Lyrical dross,
Four shades of it, smoke-purpled blue, sky-blue,
Firth's water-turquoise, is the blue chaos

Mind makes of it. Intelligence, askew,
Sunk in anachronism's precious keek
Into an everlasting Firth-wide view,

Hears timeless anger in a cart-wheel's squeak
On an old drover's road – another time,
Of the beginning emigrants, the shriek

Deep in the nineteenth century's sublime
Diaspora, when Scottish refugees
Bucked landlords, penury and sheepish crime.

Ontario and the Antipodes,
Montana, Texas, and an upside-down
Deracinated patriotism overseas,

Emerge from aerogrammes in a ghost town
Sealed by the spit of families who headed
Into salt, cast-offs of the British Crown.

Therefore that roofless ruin, rot-shredded
Rafters sprinkled among ferns and bleak briars,
Air an infertile pause where much childbedded

Women fed turf into the constant fires,
Kept up the names, filled buckets at the well,
Reared sons for work, or none, and an empire's

Nomadic armies. Graveyard of the snail-shell
And captive household botany, home to
Forgotten people, a timid harebell

Growing in shadow, now it's become pure blue
Roof, door and windows, home of open air,
Gravestone, unwritten names, memorial dew.

I had my moments in the disrepair
Time rippled into on a Firth-side hill,
Visions of then's dilapidated prayer.

Depopulated place, its physical
Selfhood was beautiful; its country shone –
Sky, water, ruins, five swans, and the still

Untimed lucidity my mind moved on.

v

What's real in suffering's not the mystique
Tragedies pump it up with. Selfish truth –
Too difficult to write, too sore to speak –

Abandons pain to poetry's lyric sleuth –
Deerstalker, pipe, and magnifying glass –
Or mid-life critic in the undergrowth

Sniffing the rhythmic stench of language-gas
While hunting down the poet on the beach
Or where he/she lurks by the underpass.

Sorrow, delight, and mysteries of speech
Turned on a sentient metre, flatter us.
What has a decent poetry left to teach?

It can repeat, describe, bespatter us
With not-being-Shakespeare-Milton-Byron-Keats . . .
Don't ask for flight. New poets are apterous.

Post-this, post-that – pre-*what*? The obsolete's
Established as a form (like this), parodic
Purloining of a thirteenth-century beat,

Dante's drum-kit, a metronomic tick,
While those intent on being 'of the Age'
Doodle devoutly in a Bolshevik

Modernist manner's nervous prose, a rage
Easy to sympathize with, but harder to
Believe (impossible, in fact), no gauge

For being alive in 1992
When life seems threatened by the very nasty
And an Apocalypse chirps *Peekaboo*

Through fissures in the sky, that very vasty
Surrounding substance of the sun and stars.
Toast Hell in Scotch, then gargle well with Asti!

Incinerated loves and burnt memoirs
May well remember quaffs like these
On speechless evenings of the grievous jars

When sorrow's nib sipped comfort from the lees
But thought it dipped in the Pierian Sink
Instead of grief's deep cistern of litotes.

Sorrow comes out, and then goes down to drink
As shy gazelles do in the wildlife films,
Poking their noses in capricious ink.

Creatures are perfect. They don't need pseudonyms.
They can't tell lies. All their events are true.
Full force of memory, before it dims –

The weight of wisdom dwindles into dew.

Back to the point, although I doubt if point
Can be the term, and so I think will you
Consider after-life delusion's vaunt.

Some have their landscapes for that big to-do
Few folk believe in, or hope for when they're dead.
'When I die, I would like to go to . . .'

How often have bedside-sitters heard *that* said
In voices dying simplifies with truth?
I think my father's was his garden shed.

They speak from innocence, in tones of youth
From a white and retrogressive deathbed-land
Where nothing's worried, guilty or uncouth.

Mine might be a certain starlit headland –
I feel silly saying it, but there it is,
My very own unnecessary zed-land.

The dream you die into, whatever it is,
Infinite leisure, or a religious
Promise well kept, or brilliant, effortless

Sex, tennis and Montrachet, can comfort us
Immensely, the eternal winning try
At Murrayfield, a long kick's fictitious

Glory made literal for ever. Why,
Anyone could get to like a Paradise
Devoted to the ego's pastimes. We'd die

To get to where imagination's lies
Come true, where who you are is who you want
To be or what you'd like to fantasize

In a perpetual hour-glass that you'll haunt
Siftingly, until you're very bored, dogged
By people like Dante and Billy Beaumont,

Big blokes who'll knock you down, or have you flogged
For not being up to scratch, Pastor Jack Glass
And Christians who *will* have you catalogued

In one or other less-than-paradisal class
Fit only for the kitchen's out-of-bounds
Or scissoring a lawn's celestial grass

While they and people like them ride to hounds.
No, make mine pagan, please, Republican,
Domestic, set in very private grounds,

A spacious grave where all five senses quicken.

VII

Oblivion, eternal zilch, demands
Heroic pluck, if that's what you have faith in.
Those personal, very private Never-Lands

Construct nirvana. Don't think – imagine!
It won't be good for you; and there are days
When I believe in grey rivers and boatmen

In shabby cloaks. I got stuck in a maze
Once in a Wonder Book. My pencilled line
Just couldn't get me through fifty wrong ways

To reach the treasure. Talk about serpentine . . .
False trails led crookedly to Minotaurs.
Whoever drew it was a loathesome swine

For whom a puzzle meant locking all doors,
Switching lights off, worse than Madame Tussaud's
Nasties in her Chamber of Horrors.

We'd all refuse a blindfold at our gallows,
Stakes, guillotines, or kneeling at the grave
Dug by ourselves, spading a life's shallows

After the paths we chose to walk, and pave
With good intentions, proved deplorable.
So, carry on, pretending to be brave;

A tear or two is quite forgivable.
Get that over, and then get over it;
But don't forget your guilty, culpable

Ethical errors – remorse is infinite.
Wrong perhapses, wrong noes and wrong yesses
Don't half increase a moral deficit –

Pissy, isn't, it, when sin's caresses
Smother you with sick kisses? It's shitty.
Involuntarily, life evanesces

Into famous last words, the nitty-gritty –
'Bugger Bognor!' 'I want a Forfar bridie!'
And other specimens of witty pity –

'Ach, only one man ever understood me,
And he didn't either.' 'A *double* Scotch,
For God's sake! Where's my fags and ashtray?'

A de-pulsed wrist with its still-ticking wrist-watch
Presents how life goes clocking ever onward
While someone's laughing on the street, your crotch

Itching as if with disrespect, swear-word
Of your own body, sacramental curse
Crossed with the secular, and both absurd —

An undertaker farting in his hearse.
Come, cancer, coronary, firing-squad;
But seldom in these several lines of verse

Speak ill of Him, monosyllabic God.

VIII

'You thought you'd died? You thought you'd really
                                                    died?'
Says a cheeky biographer, who knows
More than he should of vanity and pride.

His subject's lyric loves turn into prose.
Diaries! Photocopied indiscretions!
Nightmare, scholarly scenarios!

All that privacy, the famous reticence,
Printed! Transmitted secrets! Microphoned
Betrayals, squalor, sloth, lust, dalliance,

Become posterity's testosteroned
Chapters in which the reader gasps and laughs.
Footnoted bottles — *oo-ya*! — and he's a boned

Kippered cadaver whose recorded gaffes
Might leave you thinking you're as bad as he was —
Blared, blurted, broadcast inner paragraphs! —

And offer up a late, heartfelt applause.
What's much more likely is you'll think you're better
Or victim of a justifiable cause

Of bad behaviour, being a go-getter,
While X was passive, Y a dolt, and Z
Pathetic. There was nothing could unfetter

That proud, demented sod. Now that he's dead
Judgemental majesty sits in its court
And gives the prurient the go-ahead.

Posterity? It's literary sport.
It's sordid literature, counting maggots
Before it rubber-stamps, or not, a passport

To the critical glades, kingdom of wits
Perfect in life and work. Oh, dearie me! –
Poetry's after-life, controlled by shits.

Parnassus! Helicon! Don't weary me
With 'reputation', 'text', 'context', or 'fame';
Don't '-ize' or '-ism' me; don't 'theory' me –

The consequence of poetry is shame.

IX

Sundry tawdry wee filths, etcetera,
Mendacity, adultery, and drink's
Magical transport to its Riviera

(Though you're transformed into an androsphinx)
Could see you written down by chatterboxes;
And *there's* your after-life – high jinks, *low* jinks,

Your gluttonies portrayed as paradoxes
Frogmarched across pages. Shame is the spur!
What's left of you gets filed in little boxes.

You're in a big one, though. A character,
Fictitious now, you're up for grabs.
God help you if there's nothing there to slur,

Byronic naughties, pox, or other scabs
For posthumous picking, Burnsian pranks,
Elopements, opium, and nocturnal cabs

To roister-houses where the lady spanks —
You're guaranteed remembrance if you're bad!
Biography loves roués, twerps and cranks.

Who'd read about a saint, when there's a cad
To entertain the literary punter's
Ethical tastes in tales of Jack-the-Lad?

Wordsworthian paternity chunters
In fat books. I feel sorry for Wordy,
Hunted down, and nailed, by the truth's head-hunters.

Boring Wordworth, his morals weren't sturdy,
Or so the story seems to say, performed
On howling truth's censorious hurdy-gurdy.

Denunciation's dirty ear feels warmed
By damnatory music's dissonance
Through which the mind's informed, or misinformed,

It hardly matters which. Truth prints its licence
Much as lies do. Biography's imagined.
Subjects can look conspicuous by their absence.

If there's an after-life, it's in the mind
Of anyone who thinks about the dead
With what respect or disrespect's examined

By knowledge. There are people in my head
Whom I shall never see again or talk to
Although I dream of what they *might* have said

When I appeal to what they'd have me do
In a crisis, when making a choice
Means I might need advice to see me through

A pickle they would understand – *that* voice
No longer in the world, though I can make it
Happen so very easily, so close

It's closer than in the room. I fake it;
That's after-life, and though there might be more,
I wouldn't want to try to William Blake-it.

I have my ghosts to see. Intimate lore
Rides out from curtains over puddled light
And feels expected when a draughted door

Opens on emptiness. Unvoiced *Goodnight*
Propels its micro-whisper's spectral bye-bye
Into my head, and gives me quite a fright.

Worst soundtrack possible – seeing your life's sigh
Mirrored, re-echoed indistinct remorse,
A big noise on the spirit's glassy hi-fi –

But once you've heard it sobbing itself hoarse
In your own throat, and then let that hundredth
Nightmare exhaust its visionary force

In your nervous system, its dismal myth
Informing part of you, *that's* when you own
Your miserable life entirely. Sackcloth.

Mineral loneliness. The hour of stone.
A boat cut loose. Not much to steer it with.
Grey branches hanging over Acheron.

Look to the living, love them, and hold on.

III

Moorlander

His name began in legend at
No fixed address, next door
To hawthorns and a twisted birch.
His ancestry's recorded in
Absent chronicles, the unresolved
Transactions of his name and place,
And not in Edinburgh, nor
In any parish register
On or off the Scottish map.
Parentage and where he came from
Are as mysterious to us
As a whaup's dreams, witherty-weeps'
Pluvial metaphysics.

His body aches with footsore wilderness,
Burghs, streets, firths, seasonal miles
To cities seen at night from high places.
Strath, carse, mains, bal, mearns, dun, pit, auchter,
For, easter, wester, kil, drum, inver, aber, inch –
He runs like silent ballad, rumour, or
Black water, plotting courses by
Star-fix, fragrant month, and distant farms
Whose lights chink from a curtain or a door.
He is map and shadow – *brae, law,* and *ben –*
That fast corner of darkness
That was on the edge of the headlamps.

Scholarly trackers stir
Embers, maukins' bones,
Plucked feathers from a stolen hen.

They miss him by day and weeks.
He is downwind of their civilization.
They stalk him with tape recorders,
Cameras and disappointment's notebook.
In three languages, he impersonates
Water, gersie brae, swan, laverock,
Sionnach, curlew, and dòbhran.
He can go as an earth-trout.
He is as hoof, paw, and stealthy wing.
He can turn into tree or rock;
In winter he sleeps as such
Camped on misfortune's moorland.
Bog-cotton, tormentil, and the upland rose,
These, too, are in his repertoire,
His transformations, his metamorphoses.
Tread carefully; you don't know who they are.

Nomad, pity's statistic,
He journeyed into back-time, a ditch-lord's
Anachronism. Time turned into place.
Society gave up its ghost,
Geography its nationhood;
He put on hodden grey and climbed
Into resistant solitude.
He is the man without windows and doors.
His furniture is horizontal,
Stone, turf, or fallen timber,
Or it is the ground's hammock.
His windows are yours and mine.
Also his doors.

Infinity's emigrant,
The man who was here first
Before the road west awa' yonder

Opened America, he stirs
Mythical brose
In his fern-roofed pantry
Above an oat-coloured firth
And its high shroud of conifers.
Dusk falls with a relish for rest and beauty,
As always, as something eternal
That knows no defeat or controversy,
As sunrise, a taken-for-granted
Sameness of self with the weather.
His is the sole, licensed fire
On the hillside, a flickering smeddum,
A relic of what once was merry.
West awa' yonder, south awa' yonder . . .
Spirit at home now, indignant,
Exhausted, our new-minted ferlie –
> *'Tis this I hope and dreid,*
> *Man is enchantit to the deid'.*[1]

1 Lewis Spence, 'The Ferlie'

The Crossroads of the Birds

High on the draining ridges, a road is blue
Reflected puddles for a laverock's
Mirrored lyric; and he is here, the true
Beggar, ancestral and unorthodox.

It is the time of the crucifix, old
Pre-Reformation days and a bad year
For war; the hairst is sour and thin, and its cold
Tenantry deaf to stonechat and wheatear.

Men with steel hands are riding on this road.
He hears them miles away, then sniffs the rain
Approaching through a lowered warmth as cloud
Covers the sun, and it begins again –

A supplicant, his head hooded, his hand
Held out towards the narrow thunder's roar,
The other on his staff. Summer moorland
Tilts into scented space and a downpour

Where three roads meet. Braked hoofs and fisted reins
Fill the snort-broken silence, trampled mud,
Tapped breastplates, an equestrian fragrance
He speaks into from mortal solitude . . .

He feels his hood pushed back as a cold sword
Prods through his hair, so that the man they see
Where three roads meet above a gurgling ford
Stands eyeless in his whiskered beggary,

The stretched skin stitched, religious needlework
Peformed by Black Friars in the Canongate.
After the screaming blaze, a painful, dark
Survival. Hunger, footsteps, miles, narrate

Disfigured life that cannot see itself,
Alert in other senses. 'Wairdwood! Which way,
Blind man?' Fierce joke. A thrown penny's pelf,
A muddy coin, a mutilated day.

'Over the ford, lords, to the forge of Wairdwood,'
He answers, pointing. 'It's two saddle-hours
North to the anvils, and my word is good.
I promise you the road across these moors.

'God's arle, kind sirs? For charity and God!'
Laughter, then leather, horse and soldiery
Ride on with fifty noises to their road,
The startled heron at the stream, this story

Already chronicled and sung, its notes
Spreading by finch-song, passing through the air
On balladry, through narrative throats,
And told in Wairdwood long before they're there,

Told in another tongue than this, spoken by
Starlight, bog-cotton speech, told, and re-told
At the dragonflies' graveyard. Passers-by
Listen to language, sung, unbegged, unsold.

'Bare Ruined Choirs'

'To a blind student that hath the Irish [i.e. Gaelic] language, 3d.'
Cramond, *Church of Rathven*

Bird-song and running water, sounds such as
     Weather makes, one thing on
Another, rain, leaves, thatch, the wind and grass
     Breathing . . . When audible Anon
Sings to a blind man, any parish feels
     As nature's nation or
His own. An unseen miller's unseen wheels
     Quoted their stone, agrarian murmur.

What happens ends up written down. It speaks
     Inaccurate events,
False anecdotes, hints, covert verbal keeks
     Into unwritten testaments.
A nationless and local thrush sang there
     Beyond all history.
Unlettered life inscribed itself on air,
     Its song-life in a vocal tree.

Miles from your language that I'm blood and years
     Remote from, you would sense
Translated pity when the kirk's cashiers
     Assessed your sightlessness in pence
And Lallan speech, its spittle, lilt and lift,
     Already looking south
With ear and pen prepared to catch the drift
     Accented in an English mouth.

Unhappened Homer, dream-Bard, Ossianic
      Figment, Gaelic silence
Settles between each scratching of your stick
      On the bare road, stopping to rinse
Your mouth out with a line of song, disgrace
      On your extended hand,
Your three warm poor-box coins, kirk, trade, and place,
      One for each language of this land.

Big-weathered landscapes measure their laments
      In triple tongues, a plack
For each maimed witness and its discontents;
      And I am walking at your back,
Whatever your life, where, when, or what you did
      Off-history or in
Dimensionless parishes, the unrecorded
      Best left to an imagination

At a warm stretch. Your stick shall guide me there
      With a penny in my purse
By your unchosen heathered thoroughfare.
      Indigenous prosodic morse
Beats out the landmarks in its rhythmic braille
      And, with your eyes, I climb
Resentment's mountain, where a stick-touched trail
      Ends in a country west of time.

The Penny Gibbet

Wearing a badge to prove his pauperdom's
Licensed, official, therefore no disgrace
To the parish and the marching kettledrums,
But grounded deep in lawfulness and place,

He chooses where to stand, a blue-gowned man
Between the barrowed cripples and the tall
Two orphaned daughters of the cateran
They hanged a year ago. Good copper dole

That day by the gallows, as soon as death
Startled the crowds and prophesied their own –
Post-mortem charity when strangled breath
Froze in the air, a daughter's Gaelic moan

Chilling the deed. Now there are other throats
Brought here to weight the frosted ropes today.
A loyal beggar, hungering for groats
In the morning, by the guarded carpentry –

'*God Save the King*!' – transacts his livelihood.
A garrison of Union marches up
On its dynastic tread, and gratitude,
Servility and hate, chink in the cup.

Gaberlunzie

He sinks in. He lives in my mind's attic
Far gone in journeys as the clock turns back
On its centuries, each disnumbered tick
A loosening of time's events. The slack
Clockwork regresses on its moments as
His vagrancy sightsees the way it was
With gathered sorners in forgotten eras
Borrowing board by force and bread with blows.
Seventeenth-century footprints tracked in frost
Ascend in morning, skirting the hedgerows
Before the sun's touch melts the grassy crust
And ploughland browns through its de-silvered
                                  furrows.
So, as he walks this field, the man I see
Wears distant rags, stooping on his own strut
By the sloped edge of woods, for his secrecy
Demands a deep escape into the shut
Glades and gullies, wild country where he's safe
Among bracken, in his hideouts of fern –
Gaberlunzie, half-life, national waif,
Earth-pirate of the thistle and the thorn.

Nineteen-Thirteen

A couple in a single-end, one room,
One window with its curtain drawn,
Torn, dirty, and keeping out
Nothing of the rolling stock's
Incessant full employment.
Steam, noise and smoke
Disguise the blackened stone
On which the many tracks are raised.
They're bathing a dead baby in an enamel basin –
Gently, water from her cupped hand
Dipping and rinsing as she croons
Maternal lullabies.
She's bitter that her man
Should weep like this, sobbing
And spoiling what she must preserve.

Weeding a Border

Forget our scientists, inventors, and others
Working with mathematics and materials
Or minds chasing abstractions and infinity –
We are a people of expeditionary botanists.
Geology defines our minds and verse?
Rubbish! 'Stone for a stony heart' says all.
Devoutly may that infatuation be avoided.
Instead, think of our love of the leaf,
Our fathers, into whom we grow, tending
Chrysanthemums and dahlias at sunset
Beside a wheelbarrow and a watering-can.
Perfect carrots, the cold-frame, beetroot, lettuce,
Potatoes, and glamorous Byzantine gladioli,
These, too, are native, and express the way
A country's drawn to pleasure, as do also
Delicate sweetpeas, succulent runner-beans.
– *Respublica; république; la chose publique*:
Difficult issues steeped in mellow life's
Agreeable distractions, our words causing
Stammering embarrassment, unable to prise free
Beauty, bird-song, preferable politics.

Body Echoes

The man who disappeared in skylined scrub
Where stone was cut for minor bridges, byres,
Farmhouses, orchard walls (requarried for
Suburban patios or sunk to hold
Whooshed, Hadrianic banks of Motorways)
Turns out to be the same man as the one
Who waited at the milestone by the plinth
With milkchurns, where the country backroads bus
Drew up at his unnecessary wave
Back in the Fifties. Then, the man was old.
The man I saw up on the chiselled ridge
Levered his lean, athletic silhouette
Against the doors of April, entering
Yesterday's settlements, fields, streets and rooms
No longer on the parish map, erased,
Still showing, though, stone and grass residue
Detectable to eyes familiar with
The Voters' Roll of 1956.
Each is the same man as the young man seen
On Monday at a harbour in the east
Defying time and compass, where his brief
Marine appearance vanished into morning –
Sun on the Tay, an atmospheric stir,
An increase in the April temperature
As off he went on movements of the water,
On watery wheels, on blue light-stoked machines.
        And the woman I've seen, his age always,
From young to old, she walks in other districts.
North, south, east and west, fields and villages,

Cities and mountains, shed the present tense
To reconstruct a monstrous permanence.
In shops I go to, she's been seen waiting
At electronic tills that become counters
In former Co-ops in the former burghs –
Dingwall in 1926, Sanquhar
In a postponed, old, modern year, Dumfries
On any date after the ruined peace
Described as pre- or post-War, those events
Recalled by old men, celluloid and print
In towns where war memorials list more names
Than 1918's Telephone Directory
For anywhere named for biscuits or bridies
Or towns in Canada, South Africa,
Australia, New Zealand and the USA.
Used time is answerless, continuing
Its waste of life, so who and when they were
Repeat themselves, over and over again.
Light, land and water, the triple acclaim
Beauty enjoys when birded lilacs shake
With vocal loveliness and light is sung,
Try to disprove such sorrow, but they can't.
I've seen him walk at night in several places
Within our borders, and the national moon
Devoured him as he strode beyond his years
In the thistle gardens by the railway,
Someone for whom the future's worse than wrong.
He is as footsteps – *Is he? Isn't he?* –
Headed through etymologies and names,
Industrial herbage, frontier overgrowth,
Tangles of wild thorn, wilderness timber,
Into an unrecorded country that
Historians don't know of. If they do

They fear its absence of modernity,
Its unresolved remorse, its carelessness
With land and water, measuring the light
But not its beauty, nor its spirit, nor
How past and present are unreconciled
As any broken love, like theirs, and this
Hurts reason, as he does, and as she does –
Is she? Isn't she? – She is; and he is, too.
I've seen her stand outside a factory's gates
As if the gates and factory were there,
Expecting him among a booted shift –
That smell of foundries like a metal wind
Wafted from molten rose-beds, sharpened on
Industry, rent, ore, marriages and children.
Those tenements, the way they tumbled down
In the slow motion of history! –
Into the dumper trucks, as fodder for
Modernity's big fill-ins, Glasgow's stone
In buried middens where its bogles howl.

     Against the sounds of the sea, a roof-top dove
Performs its throated wooing. Much bird-song,
Chirping courtships, this twenty-fourth of March
By a window where a St Andrews garden
Shows off a bright azalea and a palm
In a Himalayan boast crossed with hot
Tropical green, a girl shaking her hands
At a sink. It has very deep sweetness,
This moment, colossal sugar, brilliant
Ambrosial light, and I almost forget
The woman I saw earlier today
From Innes's corner, crossing South Street,
When time wrinkled and the cars changed, years
Unwound themselves in a reversed photoflood.

I had no name to call. I saw a sound
And neither eye nor ear could hold it.
    Time took offence at what they didn't do
Or say or what they did or said, or else
Echoed existence wouldn't be like this
Recurrent riddle that my eyes witness
Out on the rim of who, when, where and why.
I've seen her in a muddy yard, headscarfed,
Soaked, by the door of a spectral byre, or
Heaving her weight against a frosted pump
Or beating passive cattle with a stick.
Is it in love that nationhood begins
To come out right and find the natural
In being and becoming, in politics
That take into account the land and light
And no one in the country goes unheard?
What foolish question's this, to test a mind
Perplexed by beauty and inertia?
They had no country, have not; until then
A nationality of night and day
Identifies them – intimate seasons, years,
Their duplicated journey, searching for
Each other in the mottled parishes
Where children play at hide-and-seek among
Tilted epitaphs and memorial texts
In the necropolis of skull kisses.
I think his death usurped its discipline,
As hers has done, places and years ago,
Two people who have lost their graves and names
Because of who and where they were and are.
Perpetual stories rattle like dried peas
In an old Ostermilk tin, saying the same
Perplexing fiction – 'Happiness is hard.

The ship for Canada leaves in the morning'.
They don't, and didn't, give enough to life,
Meaning each other, everyone, the big
Outline of possibilities, opting
For tears and overrated suffering.
    I've seen her on the street with sorrow's suitcase
With which I've seen her walk, sore with its weight,
Through present commerce on the Nethergate;
And seen him, too, and seen them look alike
At stations, bus depots, in public parks,
Brechin, Renfrew, Dalmellington and Keith,
A man, a woman, separated, but for whom
Patience is part of who and where they are,
Infinite longing but for mortal peace,
National halves, the woman and the man.
Reach with your hands into the dark and hold
And the rivers will flow, filled with many fish,
Sun and clean rain, and the hairst shall be good –
Perth, Selkirk, Inverness, Dunfermline –
Shadows on everywhere and Princes Street.

Swigs

I

Old drunks from years ago
Search for home
Feeling for routes beside
Winter's hedges, where stars
Balance on bald thorns.

Boots break frosted tufts
With drunken crunches.
Breath freezes behind them,
Puffed whisky-mist,
Aromatic shivers
At head height.

They have the force
Of 1950s fog,
Black-and-white photographs,
Drinkers from folklore.
Their faces are maps
To that country's
Bus-shelters, bothies,
Habitable ruins, kilns,
And street corners where
An outstretched hand's
Half-fingered woollen glove
Can grasp good coin,
Cupric, Britannic
Purchasing power
In patient stages,
Imperial nips.

II

Love-hurts, fecklessness,
'Bad character'
Or other scunners –
What tragedy
In that strange man
Whose childhood feels
Forgotten by
Mother and father?

He's asked to leave
By apple vendors,
Candyfloss merchants,
A man who sells
Small, sad antiques
(Candlesticks, postcards,
Dinky motors
That look like mine
In 1951)
And one who hawks
Taiwan raiment.
Confectionary carts'
Candy-stripes tempt
Sweet-toothed children.
'I'm sorry,' he says,
His leitmotiv.

I am ashamed
Of my country.

Dirtied radiance
Over the map's
Scandalized Here,
Now, Then, Tomorrow.
Damaged housing-schemes.
Schiehallion.
Rain-and-sodium
Inner city
Highways. Tiree.
Boarded windows.
Plump doves swallow
Gargled flamenco
On St Mary's Quad.
HIV-positive
Young addicts in
Rancid rooms where
Futures expire.
Lunan Bay.
Needles.

IV

Where did he go?
No one knows.
Or someone isn't saying.
I saw a man
In Queen Street Station.
I thought I knew the face
Beneath his face.
I came close to his name.
Bacterial time

Fed on the best of him,
Whoever he was
(*Was* it him?)
His hand held out
In its dolorous cadge,
His cup of flesh,
His half-cut sublime.

V

American golfing
Martini-drunks
Sway from the bar
And the big tab's
Plastic-carded.

A man with two cans,
One in each hand,
Sways on the street
Shouting nonsense.
But it's bitter
Claptrap, bombast,
Rough-bearded rant.

VI

In Edinburgh
Drunks accost me for
'A cup of tea, a bite . . .'
It went away, but now
It's all come back again.
These men are my age, though,
Or the woman at Waverley

Wearing two coats, holding
Several poly-bags,
Telling the travelling world –
'Ye think ye're miserable?
Juist listen tae this . . .'

Constables, one female,
Lead her away.
They seem to know her well.
And off she goes
With her story
Only she can tell.

VII

Not waiting at
A telephone
For anyone's ring
He is condemned to his
Addictive plod's
Roofless wander.

Measuring life
By domesticity,
Libraries, income
And furniture,
I've lost sight of his
Failure's status.

Malodorous
For all I care,
Moralized stink's
No judgement of
His choice of being's
Bargain basement,

Nor hers, who once
Stood in George Square
Tapping her foot
Out of time with
World, love, and her
Inept harmonica.

VIII

Talentless troubadours
By back-alley dustbins
In lanes between great streets
Devoted to commerce,
Law, insurance, fine art,
This, that, and the next thing,
Rope-belted drunks are singing
By the light of their eyes –
Tam o' Shanters, Drunk Men
Who didn't make it home.

IX

Stained-glass advertisements
For taken-over breweries –
Who remembers Blair's? –
And supped-dry distilleries,

Illuminate grey panes
As wintry sun shifts on
Primary colours.

Will this place ever change?
It's nowhere's terminus.
A red blur settles on
The wiped bar's mirroring
Wetness. Ornate woodwork
Makes here a temple to
Elderly artisans

Whose trades closed years ago.
It was in here I saw
A man forbidden his drink
And told to leave. He said,
'All I'm asking, Frank,
Is for a small refreshment.'
To which the answer was 'No.'

The same stained glass, clock, smell,
Similar stories mopped
First thing in the morning,
And no difference between
What I thought then, and think now –
The pity of bars. Pleasure.
Vernacular anonymity.

                    x

The man talking to himself
In the bus-shelter
Steps out of the shadows
And boxes, nimbly,

Thumbing his sniffing nose.
He spars with the litter basket.
'Ye shoulda seen me.
Ye shoulda seen me, son.'

Thirty years since I've met someone punchy.

The fantasy of fists.
The joy of great days.
From Linthouse to lucre.
The glory of having come down in the world.

'Ye shoulda seen me.
Ye shoulda seen me, son.'

XI

Befuddled crazies
Sip panther piss
By their bonfire.
In the morning
They will imbibe
Dry gulps, and fight
For a wet bead.

Who knows who here
In the dead quarry?
Dipso-Bacchus,
You're lower down
Than probable.
You're subterranean,
Angry, pickled.

Roadside litter
Sums up the rich
Pickings of life –
Polystyrene
Burger boxes,
Filter-tips, dropped
Periodicals.

One man's litter's
Another's life-
Support system.
Dowt-collectors
Scan lay-bys for
Emptied ashtrays,
What others drop.

Swillbellies, but
Hunting for booze
With begged silver,
Saving it up
For slurped bumpers,
A proper peg,
Sufficient drams.

How many here
In the stone glades?
Have you a home?
What chemistry
Keeps you alive
While it obeys
Death's inward drive?

How deeper down
Can someone sink
Into lost luck?

And why do pride,
Dignity, sit
On your shoulders
Like twin stone birds?

Libations, tots,
Lushy glugs
Go down the hatch.
Rotgut bevvy,
You name it, they're
Not fussy what
Vintage it is.

XII

The man who sold elasticated gremlins from two
                                        suitcases
At the St Enoch's corner of Argyll Street — 1951 —
Rowed half-a-dozen bouncing imps along his left arm.
One piece of leaping merchandise dangled from his right
                                        hand.
School cap, tie, trench-coat, knee socks, black shoes —
I was the big-eyed schoolboy, my hand tugged, hurrying
                                        past
A man we'd seen taking a deep swig from a half-bottle,
A man with odd, unusual, uninviting toys.

There was one who dressed in tails and a top hat; he
                                        tap-danced.
We'd seen him, too, against Lewis's window display,
                                        glug,
Then put his flask back in his wooden box of props.
Was it always raining? Were pavements always wet?

I liked the busker with the banjo. A man in a tattered cap
Was Glasgow's make-believe Bing Crosby. My hand was
                                                    tugged.
I saw a sailor standing on a dustbin, singing, women
Falling off heels, children, my age, outside public houses
Waiting for fathers, and mothers, or gathering empties
From which to make pennies in the Family Department.

Poor People's Cafés

Not down-and-outs,
Though some come close,
Nor layabouts
Trading pathos
For tea and bread,
But simply poor
In this lowered
Epoch, its door
Stiff to their shoves,
No easy entrance
To decent groves
Of furtherance.

Steamed spectacles
As I sit down
At the wiped spills,
Raising the tone
(Or so it seems)
Against their will.
National dreams
Have gone downhill
And there's a hoax
In every mouth,
Demented jokes
And diddled truth.

Such rooms translate
Half-lies in how
Waitresses wait
On out-at-elbow

Customers by
Puddled sills, drips
From windows. Pie,
Baked beans and chips;
Tea, sausage roll . . .
That smell of coat;
Dried rain, and a scowl
From a dead thought.

Two women brood;
Their roll-ups burn —
Smoked solitude,
Both taciturn,
Each parodies
In somewhere else;
And somebody's
Companion smells
His burgered plate
Then starts to eat.
Waitresses wait
On slippered feet.

He talks to a cup;
She stirs their tea
Then holds it up,
A wedded pity
In how they share —
Her sip, his sip;
It looks like prayer,
Companionship
In a belief
In the unknown,
Elderly grief
And most hopes gone.

Down in the dumps
Indignant notes
Compile a glimpse
Of huddled coats
And this kitchen's
Primitive broth
Where tendered pence
This twentieth
Day of the dead
Winter, transact
Important bread
And stale neglect.

On these borders
Being poor
Inches towards
Life less than meagre.
Going down, no rest
For the unendowed
And dispossessed.
A public shroud
Conceals their fall
And the public purse
Cuts wherewithal
To make it worse.

'Mister! Mister!
Fifty pence, please!
Come oan, come oan, sir!'
Our coins appease
Sore charity,
Expense of shame
And low pity.
And in whose name

But Government's
In Central Station,
Where life's laments
Offend a nation?

Low benefits
Or none at all
And that cap fits
On one and all
Who voted for
'Initiative',
That metaphor
By which they live.
The Devil's in 't,
The way they quest
For self-reliant
Self-interest.

Worse than worse is
How they flatter
'Market Forces' –
Mad as a hatter!
While they grow strong
Others diminish,
From wrong to wrong
Until the finish.
Twenty per cent?
Go, tax their breath!
Jack up the rent!
'Reform', or death!

Ideologue
And Moneybags
Loathe Underdog

And the Man in Rags,
And I imagine
A similar bitch
Calls profits in
To make her rich
From this cheap kitchen,
Where a bad smell slurs
A tawdry nation
And its treasurers.

'Financial link'?
That's what you say?
That's how *you* think?
Put it this way –
I say you stink;
You tax the poor.
'Financial link'?
What is it for?
I'll tell you. Sirs,
And Madams, you
Pretend to answers
As if you knew

The questions, but
You don't. You feel
A need to 'cut'
But not to heal.
'Financial link'?
What is it *for*?
It's how you *think*.
That's what it's for.
Six million souls
In pauperdom;

A round of doles
Till Kingdom-come! . . .

For a' that, aye,
For a' that, men
Could live and die,
The angry pen
Fall from the hand
And nothing change
In this hurt land
Until that strange
Obsession dies
And begging-bowl
Free enterprise
Goes to the wall.

Women who sit
Without a bean
Articulate
The unforeseen —
From opulence
By luck or tick
To indigence
In the bus-district,
The same scrap-heap
As shuttered shops,
That burst downpipe,
Those plundered skips.

'Leave them to root
In the litter-bin;
The destitute
Are guilty of sin.'
Death's dialect

Announces his
Sneered disrespect
And prejudice.
Grim children wait
While mother pays
And it grows late
For the decencies.

Queen February

She is no angel-wind, this
Orphan of orphans, kicked out
Thousands of years ago
From her mother's tragedies.

Poverty is all she's known,
Opulent squalor, rain-rags.
She has no complexion;
She is a child without skin

Fathered by distance on ocean.
Ancient ice, incarcerated water,
Squeaks on millennial centimetres
At the split, glacial cliffs.

She is northhood's daughter,
Victim first, now terrorist,
With her thin howls, emaciated
Chilled visions, refrigerated wrath

Broadcast on her spectacular
Bellows, her Golgothic breath.
Her special gift is to invade
Whole islands and to sweep them

To treeless hygiene, polished rock.
The government of shrubs and trees
Treats for mercy, but branches snap
Where her grey fingers throttle

And go flying as twigs become
Breakages, timber amputees
In the wintry leaflessness
Where light is a month's essence.

Distant trees on a ridge lean
In their submissive silhouettes –
Pale and sinister February,
A crippled slave-grove atop

Thrashed copses, frantic woods,
Shivering coniferous tips.
Her cries are thrawn and vindictive;
She is a hemisphere's affliction,

Its malevolent waif.
I stare into her stormy eye
And her screams crest as I call
To her – '*I am not your enemy.*'

But she is witches' laughter.
There is no talking to her; she is
Colossal unforgiveness,
Mockery, anger, hysteria,

And a man on a ridge feels raped
By this Fury, this Amazon
Giantess with icy lips,
Innumerable flaxen-haired

Lady Viking faces, her shrieks
Exploding from female Valhalla
And lifetimes and lifetimes of wrongs,
From the Siberian Islands.

I'm her momentary plunder,
A psyche to be ransacked, buffeted
By weather that begins in ice.
Her booty's like that – lives,

The men and women she enlists
Or steals. Their bones stuff her caverns.
Their spirits fly with her.
She means to cause trouble, and does.

When I get home, she's there.
She comes in by windows and doors,
Through the plugged chinks in them,
This Lucifer-girl, this rebel

From the world's sculleries and brooms,
Its pantries, dust-pans and sinks,
Its deplorable circumstances,
Hostels, hovels and addictions.

She has no bed or birthday where she sleeps
Among her countless replicas,
Her acolytes, the frozen genders;
She is surrounded by herself

In her stronghold, by cold fire-flesh,
Entwined and sobbing in her streeted caves
As a blizzard whitens darkness
And glaciers pretend to shift.

IV

Audenesques for 1960

Neither very brave, nor very beautiful,
Nor heterosexually inclined, but still, you were
My imaginary mentor, fantasy's ear
Attentive as I twaddled half-baked poetical opinions
Walking to work in Renfrew County Library.

Your voice was culled from two radio broadcasts
Informing the cadences of emulative reading
As of someone learning a difficult new language
In a country where it is rarely heard spoken,
Where, in any case, speech defects are pandemic.

You had become one of your doting readers
Before death claimed you in shadowy Vienna.
You, too, were a way of happening, tongue, teeth,
                                        larynx,
Sounding and looking like a demotic Sphinx
Devoted to an eccentric sagacity.

These make-believe walking pow-wows about verse
Permitted you to change my mind, throwing a tantrum,
Saying 'You bloody fool!', with the sinister antics
Of an aggressive and very dangerous parson.
You helped to populate my private madness.

With no one else to speak to on such subjects,
Small wonder, then, that I just made you up.
For thirty minutes of each morning we were both
Fictitious chatterboxes (except that you weren't).
You can learn almost anything if you have to.

'Listening to someone else recite one's verses,
While flattering, is also deeply painful.
Be a good boy, and don't, when I'm about,
Murder "The Fall of Rome" with your Scottish accent's
Rhotocistic R and slobbering lambdacism.'

You never knew about these pedestrian talk-ins.
How could such an embarrassing admission be spoken?
I saw you once only, on the other side of a room.
Self-confident timidity got the better of me.
Admiration is better off left on its own terms.

Strange, though, that seeing you was less thrilling
Than I'd imagined it would have been. After all,
In my repeated, highly informative fictions,
Something as good as trust had been contrived
But for my benefit only, my consolation,

Putting words in your mouth, and holding off
Intellectual loneliness. What effrontery,
Cheek, bumptiousness, and covertly malapert
Transgression on the privacy of a complete stranger!
But I can think of far worse fantasies.

For in those days it seemed that the only metre
Open to me for reading and close inspection
Was one whose ticks measured consumption of gas.
Imagination is Everyman's intimate theatre,
Biological cinema whose programmes run endlessly

Whether as willed dreams, sexual forecasting,
Or memories of what hasn't happened and never will.
Not much is discovered without its rehearsals
Welling up out of inadequacy and aspiration;
But it wasn't nice to have invented someone real.

It was our secret. I forgot to let you in on it.
Sorry. You were more than my useful friend.
Too often, the heartfelt is belated and shameful.
In this case some sort of national distrust –
Not mine, but others' – postponed it for years.

I was angered once by Glaswegians dismissing you as
'The Grand Panjandrum of the Homintern'.
Poetry has too many enemies to contend with.
'A nancy poet, not a real one; and a fake socialist'.
One genius tends to use another as a doormat.

Nationality doesn't identify 'our side'.
Muses are international, and mine is a Lady
Who speaks all sorts of languages (in translation),
Collects guidebooks, maps, timetables, menus,
Wine lists, and other hedonistic souvenirs.

So what if you were English? I speak that language,
But not its nationality; I love your poetry,
And our imaginary talks – I mean, remembering them –
Please me as proof of how imagination side-steps
Half-witted nagging about 'National Identity'.

A deep-dyed Peter Pan-like reluctance to hold hands
With simpletons, or suffer fools gladly, prevents
What I don't believe. Day-dream tutorials,
With teachers you never meet, end up as this –
Whispers with the dead. It is greatly to be regretted.

Pushing fifty, though, it won't be difficult
To avoid it in future. I'm not sorry it happened.
It's a Scottish night. I look at the still Firth.
Avuncular and kindly wordless calm
Shines on the aesthetically mooned water.

Extra Helpings

In our primary school
Set lunch was the rule
Though in Scotland we called that meal 'dinner'.
We tucked in like starvelings,
Inchinnan's wee darlings,
And it didn't make thin children thinner.

But what I liked best
Was disliked by the rest,
Rice pudding with raisins and bloated sultanas,
Stewed fruit and dumplings
In big extra helpings
And hooray for first post-War bananas!
>   *It was very good scoff*
>   *So I polished it off*
>   *A very dab hand with a spoon,*
>   *a spoon,*
>   *A very dab hand with my spoon.*

Detested mashed turnip
Gave most kids the pip
While cabbage was much the same tale.
No shortage of roots, and no hardship of greens –
After mine I ate Harry's, then Elspeth's, then Jean's,
O a glutton for turnips and kail.
>   *It was very good scoff*
>   *So I polished it off*
>   *A very dab hand with a fork,*
>   *a fork,*
>   *A very dab hand with my fork.*

I used to be slim.
I used to be *slim*!
'Look!' they say now. 'There's at least *three* of him!'
To which I reply
With a daggerly eye,
'Well, that's better than three-quarters *you*!'
But my clothes don't fit
I'm fed up with it
And the sylph in me's guilty and blue.
> *Semolina and sago with jam,*
> > *with jam,*
> *Oh dear, what a pudding I am,*
> > *I am,*
> *Oh dear, what a pudding I am.*

But I'm longing for lunch
And something to munch
Though I wish it was back in that school
When the dinner-bell rings
And all good things
Await to be guzzled until I am happy and full.
Dear God, I'd die
For Shepherd's Pie
In 1949 or 1950
When the dinner-bell rings
And all good things
Draw children on the sniff and make them nifty.
> *It was very good scoff*
> *So I polished it off –*
> > *Oh dear, what a pudding I am,*
> > > *I am,*

Oh dear, what a pudding I am,
But a very dab hand with a spoon,
A spoon,
And a very dab hand with a fork.

Preserve and Renovate

All day he's painted his fence, his gate,
As, yesterday, he sanded down the wood,
Replacing weather-rotted slats with good
Timber he'd cut. *Preserve and renovate.*
Do what you need to do, and do it now.
Mottoes like these explain fastidious hours
Spent tying up his borders' tasteful flowers –
No unexpected plants – the sheer know-how
Presented by the weedless path, squared hedge
And that blade-paddled, tended, watered lawn
Fit for a naked nymph to dance upon,
Though no nymph has, or would dare disoblige
The kirky vision of his husbandry
      Or get away with it,
    When, with his watchful pedantry,
He guards each moment of his dusk-grey privet.

He looked at me with almost-cross surprise
That I'd walked past his house four times today,
And yesterday, and though I tried to say
'Good morning' or 'Good afternoon', his eyes
Glanced with an elderly contempt at me
As if I'd trespassed on a sacred silence
Before he turned back to his mended fence
That he was painting white-as-white-could-be.
And he was right – my walks meant indolence
And curiosity; and he was wrong,
Because I saw in him ironic song
Echoing my dear father – an etched fragrance

From rubbed-down paint, glass paper, and the smell –
　　　　Stooping in overalls,
　　　Doing, and doing the job well,
Then paint and brush and perfumes in the pulse.

That is my work, though he won't understand;
Nor could my father. It's what I do,
This risk of feeling, that the sweet and true
Might be preserved, presented by my hand
Among the many others who do this
For the same sake that is obedience to
Time and experience, for what is due
To being, to be life's accomplice.
Four times today, and yesterday, I saw
His patient, steady, careful labour plod
In imitation of his strait-laced God;
But he looked like my father. I could gnaw
At that facsimile for ever more;
　　　　But I know who I lack,
　　　Not him, but that dead, distant doer
Who looked like him, who draws me back and back.

One Thing and Another

A fire was burning, and, as boys will do,
We raked that corner of the farm for dry
Combustible pickings, building it up
With sticks, tarpaulin rags, and waste roof-felt
Broken in slate-sized pieces that doused the blaze
To a flameless, stinking reek. One boy
Discovered a big can of old tractor drip.
It sat there for minutes while we dodged the smoke
In an eye-rubbing, coughing foxtrot.
I lifted up the petrol-smelly bucket.
At five feet from the spit and black smoulder,
Its flung, decanted arc ignited in
A bright industrial blast, a dangerous
Mid-twentieth-century bang. The can became
Too hot to handle. It was all live heat
For that split second before its gas hoof
Sent me up and back, singed and amazed,
Showing my ten hot blistered fingertips
In an involuntary flying pose.

Holding my daughter brings that feeling back
Through the sensation of her twist and kick,
Her hot will breaking free on a sudden
Obstinate, infant energy;
And I am up and back again to meet
That consequence of forty years ago
Ending its moment on this linked event,
Though what connects them, I don't know.

Early Autumn

Last month, by this same window, moist dusks
Closed the light slowly by summer curtains
And the eye had its space to go flying
Through glassy corners of sky, land and water.

Now it is dark and mid-September breathes
Numberless whispers. After blue sky,
Still Firth and summer's dry appearances,
Night is quick, with shivers at its edges.

Moths in the lampshades set to their *maudit*
Radiant, nocturnal manias, last gasps,
Powdery suicides on whirring wings.
They drop dead from electric interrogations.

My fingers smell of a soap that is new to me.
I should close windows, but aromatic fires
Linger from stubble burning all over Fife
And nothing's left of black daylight smoke.

An insect scribbles its white signature.
The letter 'a' can be seen through a veined wing.
Through 'a' the beginning of time can be seen,
A serpent's tongue licking around an apple.

Something begins in me; but I don't know
What it is yet. I shall try to find out.
It could be some sort of inhuman benevolence
Made of moth-powder, wings, smoke and soap.

A Game of Bowls

Hard to believe they were children once
Or in certain moods a lyrical triteness
Passes across the mind watching old men
Watching a game of bowls played by younger
Familiars on a day of green breezes.

That man's brother is named on the war memorial.
Two out of five are widowers and one
Went away and came back after forty years.
There were six but last week a man died
Reciting his nine-times table, sticking at

Nine-times-nine in an innumerate
Last few minutes of pillows and pain-killers.
Grandchildren rarely see them like this,
At their loose ends, one with a dog, another
Leaving his bench without a cheerio.

Or in certain moods it feels like half-a-tune
You can't put a name to, a spade's clink
On a stone, when you stand still, listening
To your cars and silence, then unseen children
Shouting from ten yards and many years away.

Just Standing There

It's a wooden bridge, an ordinary bridge,
A small one, on which I've stood many times,
Looking into the fast, earthy water, watching
Oddments sail by, rose-prunings from an upstream
                                                                garden,
Twigs, litter, sometimes a flower-head, observing
Waterside botany immersed, dragged, but never
                                                                drowned.
For years, though, I crossed the stream on my daily walk,
Ignoring that deep burn, or glancing at it.
Then I took to leaning on the timber parapet,
Staring into the fishless flood – or I've seen no fish
Ever in hundreds of quiet lookings, and if it dwindles
In summer, it is not by much, just enough
For an inch or two of bank to dry out, for a tuft
To lift its hair up from the tugging, onward rinse.
Insignificant, small, an ordinary wooden bridge,
It became a platform for a fifteen-minute staring
Into liquid muscle, a stamina that no one has
In mind or body – cliché of even little rivers
Or any patch of ground, stone, or man-outliving tree.
Commonplace as it is, it still took years to learn;
It took years to hear its several pitches of babble,
Watery lore encompassing tenderness and rage,
Always the same water, and never the same.
This is not an ordinary, small, wooden bridge,
I began to say to myself. It is my bridge.
It doesn't cross from reality to spirit,
But, in the middle, where I stand, leaning on the parapet,

Silent truth in me listens to a running giant
Let loose in unclocked liberty, as free as water
Drugged with its destination in the Firth and sea.
It's not my burn. Nothing like this is mine, it tells me.
And as for the bridge, it belongs to the municipality.
Reality is yours, and your spirit is your own.
Stand here, or anywhere, long enough, and you will learn
                                                    that.
It's not the stream or the bridge; it's where I stand
At a precise spot of nowhere and timelessness
Within myself, a door I can go through and be invisible
In a room also invisible or from which I come back
Without memory other than languageless noise in the
                                                    ears
Such as can be recalled clearly but never spoken.

Middle Age

It was around here in 1951
Where Pimples Pringle buried a dead rabbit
With my assistance in matters of ritual.
Either I recognize that stone
Or I want to badly enough to make it up.
We did it properly, with prayers, reverence,
A gully knife and a dessert spoon.
I catch myself rooting through the turf,
A mad archaeologist, for whom
Mid-twentieth-century cutlery means more
Than Celtic treasure or the Holy Grail.
If I find it, I'll run home with my secret trophy.
Nothing's left of our indignant melancholy
Other than this demented pathos looking for a spoon
In which to objectify itself. It's a big field,
For God's sake, but this is the exact spot —
I'm telling you, I *know*, I *remember* it!
So where, Pimples, did you drop the frigging spoon?
Why doesn't a big man-sized rabbit appear,
The God-of-all-the-Bunnies, and comfort me,
Stroke the back of my neck, present me with
An Electro-Plated Nickel Silver Spoon
And pin to my chest The Order of the Righteous Boy?
We sang 'Shall We Gather at the River?'
Which we'd heard in a movie starring John Wayne.
All those creatures, in graves dug by children.
Oh no, it's here; I'm telling you, I know . . .

Will all the people of the past come looking for me
As soon as it gets dark and I grow frightened?
I could sit here and find out. It'll be different
                                        at night.

Spanish Oranges

They strip so easily –
    I wonder why? –
Over- and under-frilly,
    No hook and eye.

Obstacle peel, you are
    Perfumed with south
And sweet as a mouth you are
    Mouth for my mouth.

Spherical word, it says
    Yes as I bite
Hispanic cabaret's
    Moorish delight.

Polyglot answers, *Si*'s
    Taste of *OK*
And a kissed, citric *Oui*'s
    Orange hooray.

Sun's nectareous south
    Sweetens my hands
And it drips from my mouth
    Plush Lorca-land's

Liquid guitars as night
    Dulcifies gender,
Succulent starlight,
    Lucid surrender.

Round fruit of the planet,
    Burst globe I hold,
The life and the love in it
    Beg to be told

Here in the north where I
    Guzzle and sip
Sensations that fructify
    Life on the lip.

Taste and the sense of it! –
    Plum, orange and peach,
Ripe melon's clean breast of it,
    Strawberry speech!

Number them all, such fruits
    Savour of life,
Love and the place of it, roots,
    Children and wife.

Garden Hints

Only a garden can teach gardening.
Better begin, then. Wilderness is best,
Raw ground for you to follow where it leads –
Don't bother if you haven't got the time –
Or else an ancient sanctuary, nurtured
Over centuries, from old tastes into yours.
Don't be enslaved by it. Instead, attend
With eager concentration to the place –
You live here and there's such a thing as change
Enabled by good work and husbandry.
Read what you can of histories of here
Until you sicken of their pain and woe,
Then you'll be happier with the present tense.
You'll find few chronicles of box-hedge, rose,
Cabbage, onion, beans, peas and artichoke.
Historians tend to miss the point of life's
Significant activities, labours
Truly of love, domestic devotions
For which reward is harvested improvements.
Few books on *these* subjects. Imagine them.
Elderly men might help with anecdotes
Raked from unselfish years of gardening
Such as you won't find in the How To books.
Live with the ground the way it is, and then,
Alert to quarters where sour winds arise,
Plant sheltering trees or build a wall
In keeping with the fabric of your parish.
Without advice from me, you'll have stretched out
On ground you like the look of, boulders which

You'll keep, stone roots to sit on and work round.
Astonishing your wife, you may have slept
Outdoors in a kapok bag, unused for years.
If she won't join you where tall grasses thrive,
Tell her you're thinking, or you feel the need
For outdoor, horticultural solitude.
Starting from scratch, that could be necessary —
A modern harvest, too, deserves its rites,
Spells, superstitions: plant a rowan tree.
A previous owner might have stamped the ground
With phoney gardening. With any luck
Gnomes and the brass flamingo will have gone
In the big van. Better for you, if he
Or she before you let the earth run wild,
Inviting your green surgery with spade,
Graip, hands and fingers, rooting out the rack,
Weeks of the ragged, earth-jammed fingernail.
Already tended in a style of new,
Then don't be lazy, make it style of you.
        Men, women, children, furniture, have gone;
Now you and yours repopulate a house.
So, labour warily. If a true hand
Tended the shape of it, your rose-tree will
Contain some of his spirit and the love
Between him and the woman who enjoyed
Cutting its flowers for her tabled vase.
Should she have been the gardener, you'll find
A feminine sensation in each rose.
Women who garden tend to leave their love
Wherever their gloved work's been done. Kneeling
Where women knelt, you'll feel the ghosts of love
Among undated plants, for gardens are
Intimate property, where previous claims

Share memories with present ownership.
Who, anyway, can own a tree, a flower,
Visiting butterflies, or a blade of grass?
In gardens you can sense the marriages
Of who lived here before, men and women,
Their private hours away without being gone.
The orphaned rose-tree mourned. Longevity! –
Work at your ground as if you mean to stay.
You'll measure life and time from that tall tree,
It's timber-ringed dendrochronology
Computing eras in its trunk, your own
Lifetime timetabled in its wooden clock.
Look after what you have. Don't be like me,
Besotted by arboreal mysteries,
Green legends and florescent narratives.
Don't turn your nose up at a climbing-frame,
Tree-house, a swing, or a gazebo where
Grannie can take her tea. A garden means
More than an introspective hour or two
For who's responsible for tending it.
It is a house turned inside out, a room
Higher than rooms, where sun shines, rain falls,
A room that's nothing like indoors, from where,
If you're lucky, you can see for miles.
    Hortus becomes a virtue if you can
Believe in what a garden teaches you.
Make it a work of love, a work of man
Befriended by the sociable and true,
Where children leave their toys, and wives their books.
Your house outside, a children-shouted shade
Where ball games batter shrubs, and little boys
Put beetles in bug-boxes, toddlers chase bees,
And the gardener's bad back in springtime

Becomes a family joke – although domestic,
Still keep a patch for mystery, where briars
Protect Priapus from the prurient
And shield his lover from offended eyes
Intent on newest things, not native classic.
For only those who know what gardens mean
Obey a garden's deities, or know
Transferred humanity has made them so
And that they always were protectors of
Days of loveliness, when flowers and fruits
Ripen according to the gardener's toil.
You'll know your gods are there when children play
Or friends are gathered on a summer's day;
And if you have a lawn,
Let it be grass kept sweet for walking on.

To My Desk

You're a mess, and no mistake.
You have no equestrian statues.
On your square, the poet Anon
Rides a stone bike on a stone plinth,
Upright but ordinary in
A pose of shorts and saddlebags,
A monument to the Unknown
Poetical Cyclist, prince of
Unswept asterisks, lost dashes,
Full stops, commas, colons, semicolons –
A hundred thousand dropped iambs,
Poetic bottle-necks and traffic jams.
Speech marks, alphabets, ampersands,
Discuss extremist liberty
In ethnic cafés. Closing my eyes,
I stroll your zig-zag lanes, breathe air
Whitened by laundry, polyglot
With chattering lexicons. Passports
Went out your windows when my mind
Invented what you mean to me.
Dud pens speak to elastic bands.
A matchbox whispers to receipts
And paperclip hugs paperclip.
My eyes roam quandaries and griefs
While your skeletal Anglepoise
Holds up its megaphone and searchlight,
Surreal and revolutionary bugler.
I lean on you; I sit at you
All day, writing and not writing,

Search your six possessive drawers,
Your hiding-places, where I find
Souvenirs of truth and conscience
Among tell-tale signs of squalor –
Fag-ash, unpaid bills, wine corks,
A finished bottle of Famous Grouse.
My nervous system's catacomb,
You are also a sewer, a dungeon
Where past life stratifies in peace
In its covert archaeology.
I could dig into that, but won't.
All those empty bottles named Quink,
A life of nibs, lead, and fibrepoints,
Civilian elbow-grease, helped by
Your solid and buxom morale . . .
I have laughed and cried over you.
You know where I am to be found,
Under a spire of words, or in
My garden or the university,
At which table in the library.
You know me better than anyone.
Thank God you're inanimate.
Praise be to High Heavens you're dumb
As carpentered timber, although
You speak to me, I speak to you.
I am yours now, or you are mine.
It makes no difference, wooden friend.

Long Ago

In a house I visited when I was young
I looked in through a partly opened door.
An old man sang 'Long Ago and Far Away'
To a rocking-horse, a friend's grandfather
Whose first-born son was lost at sea
Half-a-century before
In a ship whose name I have forgotten.

Whenever that sad song is played or sung
I'm in that house again, by that same door.
A woman tugs my sleeve. 'Come away,'
She says. 'Leave him alone.'
He sings, but he's no longer there.
The rocking-horse is rocking like the sea.
Ocean is everywhere
And the room is wind and rain.

Saturday's Rainbow

It happened that I saw it paint itself
In light and liquid. Sky
Turned into art. Original
Cloud-Constables emerged
To make new moments when
The eye's in love with wonder.
'Go on, then, break my heart,' I dared
To the big window as I watched
Sudden, shaded radiance declare
Its moist lustre, its big phenomena
Vivid with wet physics, working together
To arch across the Tay and link
Tentsmuir to Monifieth
Where people walked along the beach
At each bright, leaking root of it
Straining to hold the curve, driving each hue
Beyond the commonplace, towards perfection.
Those distant people disappeared in it
Or else they found
Intimate, legendary treasure on
Kaleidoscopic sand.

Then it began to break.
Its cylinders decayed. It vanished bit by bit –
Violet, indigo and blue,
Green, yellow, orange and red.
If only how we live could be as true
In our arrivals and departures as
A rainbow comes and goes . . .

It left its light-print on the conifers,
Its seven-coloured, seven-heavened smears;
And after seven flourishes, the sky
Departed in an optical goodbye.

Sketches

I

When water's edges ripple, where emigrant fowl
Rest among stubble and wiry tussocks,
November's drizzle wets the midnight owl
And the smudged moon reads from its feathery book.

II

I heard of a child born deaf and dumb
Whose patient teachers taught to read and write.
She wrote all day, wishing that sound would come
To add perfection to taste, touch and sight.

III

The boy in the hedgerow
Thought nothing could be worse
Than lying very still and low
In his nettled remorse.
He'd lifted speckled eggs
To his lips, and blown,
Tasting the deaths, their dregs
Yolked on his fingers, down
His chin, his jersey, cheeks –
Little naked necks,
Infancy beaks,
Opening to an empty groan,
Eternity's acoustics.

IV

It feels like love out of the deep, true past.
The moonlight interviews our eyes.
Wearing the moonlight, let us make it last,
Night after night, sunrise by sunrise.

V

Holding these berries was enough to do it
And I was in the church of stories again
Reading the register of local names
Dead far away, and no one could explain
Strange miles of war to me and years of time
Or why the woman in the hat was weeping.

VI

Not leaves, not puffed-up weightless jute, that dry
Sinuous woodland air bagged and forgotten
By whoever. Heavy even to look at . . .
I didn't dare put my hand inside;
Instead, I used my stick, and saw
Acorns, an oak wood in a sack, shovelled,
Picked up or scooped, raked by a forester's
Chipped fingernails, or gathered by
Oak grocers, distributors of groves
From occult homelands, suppliers to
Druidic cults in their scattered chapters.
I weighed it on my body which braked
In a skid of arms. We export water,
So why not autumn, acorns, fallen leaves
Or hieroglyphic daylight's pagan prayers

Scribbled on a timber sky,
Visionary, undeciphered languages?
I heard feet on the massed leaves, a scuffed
Approach expert over the leaf-hidden paths.
I ran away from the Squirrel Man.

VII

Our dappled nakedness and who we are
Turn into carnal fiction when the light
Dwindles into a single windowed star.
There is no love like ours tonight.

VIII

In the leaf-folding wind, what claw, what twig
Or what ground-toughened fingernail
Scratches the window-pane? What underdog
Begs me to save him from the gale?

Misshapen Caliban, come in, come in;
Tell me the secrets of your lost
Reality, your Pictish origin.
White music in the storm is a swan's ghost.

Here is a bowl of milk, your dish of brose.
Our kingdoms fell and they are gone;
Our names were sundered when our foundries froze.
No words are left, other than cuts on stone.

An ostracized dimension fills my house.
He is a lump of me disguised,
Dead blood, antiquity, a dangerous
Anger, impenitent, unmodernized.

'THE NAMELESS BAIRN'

'. . . the never-surfeited sea
Hath caused to belch up you.'
Shakespeare, *The Tempest*

A Scots word adds its local sentiment –
Almost-Victorian pathos –
To a drowned infant
Without birthday or accurate death
Discovered by our postman on the shore.
Raise an invisible cairn
On the murderous water
Where conscience can inscribe
Parentage and the rest of the story.
By a true grave, shed tears for
Whatever caused such anonymity.

SETTLEMENTS

Through days of mice and dust
Baled hay in tidy settlements
Preserves the harvest's reaped remains.

Here is my hedgerowed State,
My stubble republic
Lulled once by music of the breeze-blown grain
And barley's bearded whispering.

Those summer burghs! They recur
In annual, unpeopled splendour,
Straw clachans that depart at night
Into remote utopias . . .

XI

FEBRUARY 1988

At a rained-on service station, drivers stop
To fill their tanks, and, pouring petrol, stare
With one eye at a boiler-suited girl
Who, at her till, ties ribbons in her hair.

Prodigious Twins

Each evening, after tea, the seaside twins
    Performed before sofa'd and armchaired guests
Careful with their teacups as they heaved
    Admiringly in their unsavage breasts.
Their parents smiled a bit, but frowned a lot
    When fingertips fluffed notes, though no one else
Noticed these errors. I sulked, pretending to
    A serious study of Sir Walter Scott.
Their patience made you think of fortitude;
    While other children lounged at window-sills,
They sketched or read, immune to boredom.
    That boy and girl were steeped in indoor skills,
Although, in how they sat, while mother knitted,
    Four-fifths their energies seemed held in check
By a superior restraint, their mother
    Watching for signs – 'Go on, I dare you – *fidget*.'
Our selfish fathers golfed like rainproofed spectres
    Caped on the dismal links. Each white, clubbed ball
Spun round its rain-tail into drizzled distances.
    The North Sea's weather blustered, squall by squall;
Striped brollies lifted on the gusts, held fast
    On the drenched greens; or, in the puddles, a car
In the soaked gaiety of a departure,
    Waded a wipered road through the rain-pocked
                                glass.
After the great rainbow, we went outside
    To watch the summer's come-back. Water-drawn,
Those crippled rainbows in re-laundered blue
    When the weather cleared and the sun shone;

And broken rainbows all that afternoon
    As clouds moved north and the half-hearted
                                showers
Cleared putting greens, driving the elderly
    Into the shelters, twice, and then again.
I *liked* watching the ancient on the run.
    I was in my element, and in the pink,
Wanting to duck and drown Sir Walter Scott
    In a very, very deep lagoon of ink.
School-uniformed, tethered to watchful eyes,
    You never saw them other than in tow —
Black, polished shoes in that season of sandals
    And naming the sea-birds like an exercise
They'd face a test on later. Father taught,
    I'd gathered, in one of the better schools
Near Glasgow: I could just imagine it.
    Parents behaved as if their kids were fools
Compared to these two, picking up the hint
    From their propriety and flashy talent.
My mother clipped me on the ear, in passing,
    Although I sat, a literary saint,
Scowling at *Ivanhoe*. 'Far from his best,'
    The teacher-father said. The way he said it
Soured me, and then I said, 'Yes, *Waverley*'s
    Much better, but, of course, I've read it.'
I think it was 'of course' caused the delayed
    Cuff on the ear, for the giving up of cheek,
In an advanced sarcasm, was *my* forte.
    Even if all I could do was tailor-made
For silence — sitting and reading — show-off
    Useless knowledge was right up my street.
A lecture, though, on R. L. Stevenson,
    Wouldn't have entertained them, not one bit;

Nor me, either – angry, shy, and terrified
    In case my mother stood up to announce
The Pied Piper of Hamelin, my party piece,
    Doing her bit to save the family pride.
I thought they looked like twins born to succeed.
    Their sprinting fingers dazzled as they played
That boarding-house piano, four clever hands
    All over Mozart with prodigious speed,
Stunning the triple spinsters. They impressed
    Parental couples, probably bereft
Because their children lacked the skill or patience
    To turn an inclination into gift.
What pride their mother showed looked mean and
                                                        pinched.
    She hardly ever looked up from her knitting,
Her criticism coded on her needles;
    And if you looked at him, the father flinched.
My summer pal whispered: 'They make me sick.'
    I knew how Billy felt, only too well.
Calls of 'Bravo!' and 'More!' led me to notice
    Pained symmetry in that quartet from Hell.
Easily seen, how music drew them in
    To private worlds, their genders twinned in one
Immaculate and almost-abstract person,
    Harmonious, released from discipline
Into performance. Anyone could sense
    Sly self-control hide lack of interest
In fractured courtesy, indifference
    Rehearsed too often in a shaken wrist.
Other than read, all I could do was dream
    That I was somewhere else, selling these two
To the Apaches, commending the ant-hills
    And other tortures equally extreme.

My cute, befriending questions met with 'No,'
    Or '*Maybe*' hinted in an unkind pause.
They seemed to take a pleasure in these words.
    I envied them their pampering applause,
Their practised bows and dutiful encores
    Reeled off in fingered dramas, but demure
For all their energies. 'What talented *twins*!'
    A woman cried, as I made for the door.
One night, like everyone, I felt ashamed
    At what happened. We saw their lives surface
In clear story, unmusical, but named,
    An exact sensation of their futures.
At tea, I'd overheard them where they sat
    At the best table by the window,
A last, firm word closing a family row,
    Not much more than a ripple, even if that.
It didn't seem over, though; you could tell
    From how the twins stood by the piano, tense
And calculating, knowing without words
    When best to strike their discord of defiance.
Conventional and doting guests were shocked
    At that co-ordinated, double fury:
Twins screamed, and hammered four hands on the lid,
    Their father saying, 'No. Sit down. It's locked.'
'A punishment,' he said, showing the key.
    His children stamped. They made the saucers shake.
Then it was quiet. Adults stirred their tea
    With thoughtful spoons, and passed the cherry
                                            cake.

'Scenic Tunnels'
Niagara Falls, Canada, 7 April 1992

Portals open on
Cold, wet cremation.
Phenomenal essence
Thunders constantly
Against the eye –
It never stops –
And is decreated
Over and over
At the same speed's
Roaring velocity.
Infinite weight
Turns into air,
Water, haze, and blink,
But as if fire also
Plays its elemental role
In this droughtless wonder:
It is so absent
That you think of it
And you think of it
And you see white fire.
Subterranean winds
Whoosh in the rock.
Downward momentum –
It looks like ice,
Arctic power's
Venerable brawn
Crazed by falling,
The boiling bergs,
That sort of wonder –

Not one of seven
But of very many,
Some of them mine,
Some yours, some those
Of she who died
A few hours later
Outside Erie,
For I don't forget.
It is all of
Twenty-seven years ago.
With this photograph
(Three weeks later)
I hold summer
1965.
My thumb's pulse tumbles
Its own Niagara
And my eyes bubble
Looking at Maggie,
Lesley (both dead),
In printed mist's
Light-written white-blue.

Thunder, lightning,
Ice and thunder
Ice in the eye
By the cold furnace
And the yellow macs,
Everyone like children
And the blind children
Who are here, listening
Smiling as the blind smile,
Listening, unafraid.
Spectacular noise

Rumbles, perhaps
The voice of God.

God forgive me.
My old self strains
Against this new one.
The tunnel's end
Shows no light, only
Natural wrath,
White turmoil, force
Into which men cut,
Tunnelled, engineering
Forbidden glimpses
Into the heart.
Ice-smoke. Water-fire.
Horror of self.
Close a door on it.

V

Dressed to Kill

*'When I was a boy
I loved my country.'*

James Wright

I

Audible pepper
Vindaloo for the ear
Orchestra's leper
Sonic frontier
Puff, spit and ornament
Grace notes of battle
Rally the regiment
Lament and death-rattle
Xenophobia's solo
Windbag of wrath
Chauvinist's wallow
Lyrical bloodbath
Musical bonfire
Melodious shriek
Present tense haywire
When ancestors speak

II

Like it or lump it   it's part of our nation
Object to it, loathe it   admit it exists
Dismiss it as wicked   war's cultured damnation
The status quo's finest   fantasists, militarists
Detest or suspect   war's ethical swamp
Whatever your feelings   it's usually with us

National dirty work	flags, drums and pomp
Right, wrong or justified	half-wits or heroes
Political tantrums	boastful, invasive
Defended convictions	repellent, persuasive

III

Scottish landmarks, fortified,
Become geologies of pride,
Shadowy places, holding on,
Identity in weathered stone.

Tomorrow's soldiers come to taste
Arts of battle, young, fresh-faced,
Centuries locked up within
Tradition, craft, and discipline.

Fathers, father's fathers, for
Six generations marched before.
Sons, and daughters, learn to shoot,
Learn to drill, obey, salute,

Learn the regimental lore,
Ritual, ceremony, war.

With a hey tuttie-tattie and a tow-row-row

Land of Wallace, Douglas, Bruce,
Field Marshal Keith and brave Montrose,

It gave away its independence
Without a fight, for trade, peace, pence.

A land of soldiers, mind, and science,
A nation turned into a province!

With a hey tuttie-tattie and a tow-row-row

Where I come from tradition's trade
Means Old Morbidity's parade,

A time-served ethos, soldiering on
To bagpipes with a sword-tipped gun.

With a hey tuttie-tattie and a tow-row-row

Peacockish Scottish regiments
Enforced Great Britain's do's and don'ts.

Mac-scatterings of volunteers
Manned the Empire's hot frontiers,

Diasporic tartan's travelogue
Through continents of alien grog.

With a hey tuttie-tattie and a tow-row-row

Dressed in a military skirt
You'd *have* to be an extrovert!

Embarrassment or paradox —
Crack warriors in their poshest frocks.

They groom each other, taking care,
Spartans, combing their friends' hair

Before Thermopylae, the neat
Perfection of war's butcher-meat.

Dressed to kill, aesthetic Jocks —
The decorative arts *de luxe*!

Tartan soldiers, their *esprit*
Twinkles on each naked knee,

Each button rubbed until it glows,
Brushed doublets, calibrated hose . . .

Gender's awry! French hussies flirt
With secrets of a soldier's skirt

And – ooh-la-la! – but *dulce est*
Pro patria mori intumesced!

'Pour l'amour, oui; pour la guerre, non!'
Thus General Joffre – right *and* wrong.

Potatoes, chestnuts. – Hung like oxen,
Highland legends with posh frocks on.

IV

Come intae ma museum. It's a shrine
Tae sodgers o' thur country's Thin Red Line.
As yer a-followin' o' ma finger
Don't ye bluidy well malinger
Or ma doggerel 'll get ye,

up yer erse!

Ah'm a spectral sergeant-major, tak' ma wurd.
Ah'm the speerit o' the valiant 93rd.
As ye keek at each exhibit
Respec' the story in it
Or ah'll nip ye, wi' ma bayonet,

up yer erse!

Ah never caused nae wars. *Ah'm* no tae blame.
In every war thur wis, ah wantit hame.
Och, yer chunter's aw a bogey
Fur we fought demagogie
An' if ye don't believe me,

up yer erse!

Ach, ma bonny lads wur withered in the fire.
They're singin' in Damnation's Male Voice Choir.
Fourteen-Eighteen an' The Forties
We aw died in bagpiped sorties
An' oor widdas got a pittance,
                                                      up yer erse!

V

Victoria's era loved its wars
Its riflemen and *beaux sabreurs*
Its Highlanders, its Lancers and Hussars
        But Balaclava's blunder
        Filled Tennyson with thunder
Which he dandled on the dactyls of disaster
The poetry of Empire in full cry!
There was nothing that it wouldn't versify
For commerce, conquest, love of war, and fame

        Sir Colin Campbell's soldiers made
        A very decorative Brigade
Kilts, sporrans, bonnets, tunics, spats and hose
        Romantic even then
        Those Highland riflemen
Designed for poetry and not for prose
42nd, 79th and 93rd
And they doted on Sir Colin Campbell's word
For wages, grog, the love of war, and fame

SIR COLIN CAMPBELL: 'There's no retreat from here,
    men! You must die where you stand!'

SOLDIERS: 'Aye, aye, Sir Colin, and needs be, we'll do
    that!'

[133]

SIR COLIN CAMPBELL: 'Ach, 93rd! Damn all that
eagerness!'

Or so the surgeon overheard
Among the Highland 93rd
What made nine-hundred men do what was dared?
Don Cossacks and Hussars
Equestrian sons of Mars
They, too, were dressed to kill and well prepared
If battles must be, let them be like this
For grown-up causes and civilianless
Though they were there for politics and fame
No, don't debunk them. Underfed
No change of clothes, no tents, no bread
Dysentry and cholera and scurvied skins
While 'Kindly Billy' cut
Through stumps and wounded gut
Diseases made a bumpkin of his medicines
In Balaclava's church the starving sick
Lay down to live or die and prayed in Gaelic
For food, clean linen, warmth, or death and fame

VI

Who marched to war in scarlet coats
With kilts, spats, hose and feather bonnets
Now dress to look like grass and trees
And are forbidden naked knees

With a hey tuttie-tattie and a tow-row-row
They've raised Culloden on the radio
Camped out like great-great-great grandfather's dad
Or stragglers from a Scottish Iliad

A military nation, but
For all its regimental glut

No MacNapoleon, no dictator,
Few ideologues, no liberator!

With a hey tuttie-tattie and a tow-row-row
Not Bonnie Princes but Geronimo!

VII

    Victorian ferocity
    Respectable atrocity
White women and their children were at stake
    Rapes were few, if any
    Murders, there were many
So they drove the bayonet home and no mistake
Death-drudgeries of governance and gibbet
Where nothing could be done without a chit
And they blasted mutineers across the guns
    Their wrath was Caledonian
    Crossed with the Tennysonian
And like Puffed Wheat they shot them from the guns

    Sir Crawling Camel's 93rd
    Looked at the breach and undeterred
By what a little breach it was, they charged
    Lucknow's breached Sikanderbagh
    Smoked beneath the British flag
Sikanderbagh was well and truly Raj'd
And little Drummer Grant, fourteen years old,
Charged too: he didn't do as he was told
    They found him struck down dead
    And his wound was red on red

A hero-child among those men who charged.
The gardens rattled, bloated vultures rose
From buttons, buckles, badges, bones of those
Who'd died in battle, not across the guns
        Allegedly superior
        To vengeance's hysteria
But those not shot or hanged were blown from guns

VIII

When I've stotted back from my work on the farm
        I undo the leathers and hang up my arm
And then I unfasten the straps of my peg
        To look at the nothing that once was my leg

These days I just manage as best as I can
        It's left-handed work but I'm still a man
Sir William the surgeon has made me upright
        But he can't take away what I think of at night

A Cameron Highlander's hung on the wire
        He's missing his head and the rest is on fire
Machine guns and shrapnel are razoring sky
        But the silence I hear was once a man's cry

They allow me to potter about on the farm
        It's sore on the stumps of my leg and my arm
I've ointments for each but it's left-handed work
        Though far rather that than a plaque in the kirk

We were all tartan turnips in poisonous muck
        The pipes and the pipers were shot aw tae fuck
The Archies and Alastairs, Frasers and Jims
        A half-buried litter of helmets and limbs

Right arm and right leg, I'm a lop-sided veteran
    There's far worse than me in the war-bield of
                                   Erskine
With two wooden fists, he's survival's élite
    When he's out for a stroll on his two phantom feet

Their soot has got into the weave of my clothes
    Like soot from a bonfire that smirches a rose
Their particles lodge in my eyes and my hair
    And I saw the dead Camerons enter the air

But I was half-cloven and not smithereened
    A child of my time, I was nineteen-seventeened
I feel myself withered, or halved, or unborn
    Impaled on the point of the century's thorn

On highways of time, on crutches or pegs
    Soldiers and sailors have nursed their lost legs
Pensioned or begging, for hundreds of years
    Limp cannonballed tars and gunned fusiliers

Fa-la-la dee, diddle-dee, I'm still frisky
    With left-handed fag and left-hand poured whisky
But sometimes I dream when I'm stretched out in bed
    Sir William Macewan has cut off my head

IX

I grew up a mile from Erskine Hospital, which is on the
south bank of the Clyde, west of Glasgow.

    I saw a man with no legs. He was in a wheelchair
which was pushed by a friend who was blind.

    I dreamt I met a man with no head. He spoke to me.
He had a mouth on his chest. Or was it a button?

    Or a medal?

Erskine Hospital opened in 1916. After the battles of the Somme, hospitals couldn't cope with the numbers of limbless soldiers. Or limbless soldiers couldn't cope with the lack of hospitals. Or with the lack of limbs. Or whatever.

Erskine specialized in artifical limbs and rehabilitation. Tradesmen from Clydeside shipbuilding put their skills to a new craft of prosthetics. 2,697 limbs were fitted by 1918.

7,000 tons of cotton wool were used by the Royal Army Medical Corps in the Great War. Can you imagine even one ton of cotton wool? – A county covered in snow. How many times round the globe would the bandages of modern wars wind, allowing room to tie them in a big, global bow? The planet's ribbons are white, with red seeping through.

More than 22,000 artifical eyes were needed. – A town of one-eyed men. A village of men with no eyes at all. Ocularists were the unacknowledged war artists. A lot of their clients couldn't see what they hadn't commissioned.

Erskine appeals to a good and generous public. It *ought* to have a good and generous government.

That isn't meant to be political.

It's just meant. Pure and simple.

But if Erskine Hospital depended on a government, it would probably be underfunded, cut, or forgotten. Who'd want that for a game of soldiers?

When I was a boy, and still loved my country, there was a man in Erskine who'd been at Omdurman. There were several who'd fought against the Boers. Now only a few are left who fought in the First World War.

Mr Archie Stewart is such a man. He spoke of how patriotic duty led him to join the army while still under age in 1914. He also spoke about Passchendaele.

X

Not many of you left to tell the tale
Of that apt, horrid place-name, Passchendaele.

Perdition's masters, in their big châteaux,
Pored over maps and felt their whiskers grow.

Field Marshal You-Know-Who's baronial 'tache –
Trimmed by an orderly to cut a dash!

Horse-booted pose, the military whisker,
High Jingo to a Kiplingated air . . .

Mr Chas. Niblo spoke of how, in the 1920s, he explained to a recruiting officer that he wanted to join the Army because he was starving. He spent many years in uniform.

XI

When Niblo shouts, you stand up straight, by God
You do. Pity whoever mortified
His Regimental Sergeant-Major's pride
Or stood in Mr Niblo's Awkward Squad.

But hard-earned pride – a Scottish orphan's skip
Into a family and membership,
Then years of duty, logged *Exemplary*:
True to his salt, and three square meals a day.

Mr James Shields spoke of how, in 1944 in Normandy, he'd suspected some soldiers of the Glasgow Highlanders of running away, instead of 'going back for stores', as they claimed. He offered them a choice of a court martial, or returning to their battalion. They opted for the latter. It crosses his mind still if he sent them back to die.

XII

It's not all Scottish butch *élan* –
Though thousands fought, some also ran.

A French philosopher once said
That long before he's shot down dead

The rational soldier drops his gun
When sanity says, 'Run, Boy! Run!' –

Intelligent armies run away
And live to run another day;

But it's well known, Inferno's Gals
Are seldom intellectuals,

While intellectuals are rarely
Good at facing gunfire squarely.

Ladies from Hell, their danders up,
Steeplechasing at the gallop!

Assault course? That suggests attack.
Good practice, though, for running back

To cosy, comfy, sandbagged boozers
Bullet-proofed for battle's losers.

Going gets tough, the tough get going?
Where to-ing is, there's also fro-ing.

Is it brain, or gifted brawn,
Drives ordinary soldiers on?

No just sore parade-ground blisters
Wearing skirts much like their sisters' –

These 'work experience' trainees
Might have to think of good degrees

For PhDs home Smart Bombs in
By very fancy navigation,

Technologically epic,
Algebraic, phallic, slick

Computerized destruction's strut,
An electronic uppercut.

They wait for green at traffic lights,
Read the citizens their rights;

In through cat-flaps, up the stairs,
Respectful of civilian prayers,

They wipe their feet, apologize,
Pulverize, and atomize.

*With a hey tuttie-tattie, the Thin Red Line
's been wiped out by a Claymore Mine*

Few HRPs[1], but still vexatious,
Gopping, goopy,[2] and hellacious;[3]

Scores of most Unhappy Teddies[4]
Trembling in beshitted Shreddies[5]

When the Very lights soar high
Into an exploding sky.

A night-sight's lunar battle-view
Turns everything to nightmare blue . . .

Blue sand, and blue the sweat that drips,
Blue triggers and blue fingertips . . .

Updated trig and bombardiers
Reduce the enemy to tears.

Art meets science, War meets Wealth,
Come up with morbid sculpture – *Stealth*:

Vampiric, bat-like, secret, deft,
And named for subterfuge and theft.

Equestrians set forth to prick
On plains of Nineveh. Iraq,

Ruled by its lunatic Caliph,
Twice-steeped in sabre-rattlers' grief,

Courts the fate of Babylon,
Mesopotamia's bridges blown.

1 HRP: Human Remains Pouch
2 British Army coinages, meaning 'Bloody awful'.
3 US coinage, meaning obvious.
4 British Army slang for 'highly discontented soldiers'.
5 British Army slang for 'string underwear'.

Sammy's[6] no Saladin. Failed Faust
Refused to mount, ride out, and joust,

While Stormin' Norman, at the gate,
Did Swordplay for the Overweight.

New Jersey's tribune saw it through
With planning on a VDU –

Maps, tons of scientific bumph,
The hush-hush paperwork of triumph.

Hi-tech sky-jockeys zero'd in
On a highway's charnel chicken-run.

Modern, boffined war still means
More than multiple machines

But soldiers, who, with bayonets,
Clean up the aftermath of blitz . . .

Help the wounded and surrendered,
Plastic-bag the pulped and squandered.

*With a hey tuttie-tattie and a tow-row-row
'Friendly Fire' is Slaughter's Sorrow*

Few losses, but they're sorely felt
For being few, as sorrow's lilt

Laments misfortune's fusiliers –
Audible sorrow, audible tears.

*

For someone born in '42
This subject sticks like rancid glue –

6 British Army slang for Saddam Hussein

All those wars, before and since . . .
Rinse hands, and rinse, re-rinse, re-rinse,

But still the blood just won't wash off
As if the world can't get enough.

Excuse my piety, but trust
My double-edged, two-faced disgust,

For history is immature,
Or maybe I am, or you are.

*

Raving, Tabloid Peter Pans,
Our automatic partisans,

Drool for patriotic battle –
Hear their paper sabres rattle.

No, by Jingo, no, I'm not
A patriotic *British* Scot

Although I was once, doting on
Indigenous print-outs on stone

Naming the names, the long-ago
Juvenile eras of sword and bow,

Homeric poetry, the shield
That for a child's war armed the child[7]

Against the redcoats tramping down
Bonnie Prince Charlie's heather crown

Or Edward's armoured finery
When Wallace cried out, 'Don't be fley!

7 Randall Jarrell

You're in the ring. Now dance with me!'
To die in a schiltron's liberty!

The patriotic puddle's a sink
Where racial monsters come to drink.

Mischief, duty. — Aye, ambivalence.
Rinse hands, rinse, re-rinse, re-rinse,

And if the blood still won't wash off
Maybe it's me can't get enough!

XIII

This painting's a heroic thrill
That stirs my blood, and always will —

The Thin Red Line above a mantelpiece
Defeats my pacifism, and strikes me dumb —
The glory that was kilt and riflegrease,
The grandeur that was bayonet and rum.

    Ironic sepoy. *Whaash my nashun*?
    No answer. Silence's oration.

    With a hey tuttie-tattie!